"Dudley Hall's ongoing ministry of refreshing and rich revelatory insight into God's Word is a constant source of blessing to many. I praise God for this contribution to all of our enrichment and growth as believers."

DR. JACK HAYFORD
SENIOR PASTOR, THE CHURCH ON THE WAY, VAN NUYS, CALIFORNIA

"At the touch of a finger, we can communicate with people around the world, yet it still seems that communication is our greatest weakness. It is my personal conviction that it all begins with our failure to effectively communicate with our Creator. There is static on the line, and the clear channels seldom seem to be in place. God help us! This is what I believe He is seeking to do through Dudley Hall in his book *Incense and Thunder*. Dudley wants to help us learn how to communicate effectively with the One who knows the answer. He can help us clear the channels, discern the voice of God, and move into His abiding presence. I'm convinced, as Dudley will point out, that it must begin by communicating and interceding with God—and not only letting God hear our hearts, but staying in position to hear God's heart."

JAMES ROBISON
FOUNDER, LIFE OUTREACH INTERNATIONAL

"Dudley Hall is one of my favorite teachers in the body of Christ. His new book, *Incense and Thunder*, is at once both practical and inspiring. It will reward its readers by deepening their confidence in the power and pleasure of prayer."

JACK DEERE
AUTHOR OF *SURPRISED BY THE VOICE OF GOD*

"This is the finest work I have ever read on power with God through prayer. This man of integrity deserves to be heard."

PAUL CAIN
SENIOR AUTHORITY, SHILOH MINISTRIES
AUTHOR OF *WORD AND SPIRIT*

"Incense and Thunder is a much-needed book. It's emphasis on intimacy and power with God through prayer is vitally needed. Everywhere there is a renewed interest and emphasis on prayer. Without some guidance and help, people will soon see prayer as fruitless. This book, simply and without too many words, deals with one of the greatest hindrances to prayer—self-righteousness—and with the greatest help—Spirit-guided prayer. I encourage people to apply these needed truths in relation to prayer so that intimacy may be received from Him and His power released through us."

PETER LORD

AUTHOR OF *HEALING GOD*

Incense & THUNDER

Experience Intimacy and Power

with God through Prayer

DUDLEY HALL

Multnomah® Publishers *Sisters, Oregon*

INCENSE AND THUNDER
published by Multnomah Publishers, Inc.

© 1999 by Dudley Hall

International Standard Book Number: 1-57673-482-X

Cover design by Kirk DouPonce
Photo of praying hands by Colin Faulkner/Photonica
Photo of clouds by Robert Clemens/The Image Bank
Photo of lightning by Weatherstock, Inc.

Scripture taken from the *Holy Bible, New International Version,* © 1973, 1978, 1984 International Bible Society. Used by permission of Zondervan Bible Publishers.

Also quoted: *New American Standard Bible* (NASB) © 1960, 1962, 1963, 1968, 1971, 1972, 1973, 1975, 1977, 1995 by The Lockman Foundation. Used by permission.

Multnomah is a trademark of Multnomah Publishers, Inc., and is registered in the U.S. Patent and Trademark Office.

The colophon is a trademark of Multnomah Publishers, Inc.

Printed in the United States of America

For information:
MULTNOMAH PUBLISHERS, INC.
Post Office Box 1720
Sisters, Oregon 97759

99 00 01 02 03 04 — 10 9 8 7 6 5 4 3 2 1

A belated thank you...

Miss Lily Barnett lived between our house and the little country church we attended. Her husband had died years before, and she didn't drive. My folks always picked her up at the picket fence gate to take her to church.

It was my responsibility to open the car door for Miss Lily. We picked her up early on Sunday for Sunday school and worship and on Wednesday night for prayer meeting. Each time I opened the door for her, she would say, "I'm praying for you. I pray that God will call you into the ministry." That wasn't what I wanted to do, so I don't ever remember saying "thank you."

Oh, did I mention that at age seventy-five she also volunteered to teach the Royal Ambassadors (the Baptist young men's organization)? There were only four of us, but she was faithful to meet each week to teach and pray for us.

Miss Lily was never famous among men, but she made a huge investment in my destiny. I have been in ministry for thirty-two years. Now I want to say to Miss Lily, "Thank you!" Thank you for praying even when your subject didn't appreciate it. Thank you for believing in a big God and a little boy.

Also, I want to say thanks to my father and mother, who cared enough to stop for Miss Lily and who also prayed for their children daily. Prayer was natural for Mother, and Dad never prayed aloud without his voice breaking with emotion. Thank you both for being a living prayer for me. You have left me a great heritage.

CONTENTS

NORMAL LIVING

The drought was terrible. It hadn't rained in thirty long years. Crops had failed. Livestock had died. The banks were closing their doors—no more credit. The meteorologists were offering every explanation they could think of to explain the extended drought that was devastating an entire nation and affecting the whole world.

There was an explanation: "Elijah...prayed earnestly that it would not rain."[1]

CENTURIES LATER...

They had locked up that fanatic zealot. He was causing all kinds of trouble. He just wouldn't let it die. He kept stirring up the people talking about that Nazarene who had been crucified some time earlier. He even insisted that the Nazarene had come back to life and was still performing miracles. But they had him now. In jail...that's where he must be kept until this sect got over its period of denial and things settled down again.

Embarrassed! The jailer reports to the sergeant that the zealot is gone, but the doors are still locked. How could this have happened with their tightest security? Rumors are rampant. People are losing their jobs, even their lives, as accusations of treason get louder.

Again, there was an explanation: "Prayer was offered to God for him by the church."[2]

These trials are just normal, everyday life for those chosen to represent heaven on earth. They know that heaven and earth are connected by the Creator and His purpose. Nothing on earth can be fully explained without heaven's perspective. And nothing is impossible on earth if heaven grants it. The whole idea is to get what's happening in heaven to happen on earth. God has chosen to accomplish that through designating His sons and daughters as ambassadors who intercede through simple prayer.

The real explanation to the events of history is not written down in our history books. Make no mistake! It *is* all being recorded—just in another book. The real explanation in the end will have a whole lot more to do with who prayed than who presided.

The power that directs the affairs of this world is wielded by the faith of those who know the King. His reign is absolute. He has given us (believers) the privilege and responsibility to enforce His kingdom of love in the earth. He waits until enemies such as hate, pride, prejudice, greed, and slander are vanquished by love. This kingdom is advanced as the subjects learn to live in a state of constant communion with Him and pray, "Thy will be done on earth as it is in heaven."

We send up the incense. He sends down the thunder.

CHAPTER ONE

PRAYER: FIRST IMPRESSIONS

Prayer meeting! As a boy who attended a rural country church, these words didn't conjure up hope for an exciting event. I went, and it was not much fun for a kid. There would be some community discussion, and then someone would give a small devotional talk that seemed mostly irrelevant to me. Then we would bow to pray. Each would take his or her turn. I knew how everyone would start. Mr. Jackson would begin with "Most wise and merciful Father," then go on to cover some of the needs in the church family. Mr. Franklin would start, "Our Father who art in heaven." Everyone had their own style. Before it was over, most all the sick and needy had been prayed for, the pastor had been "held up" before the Lord, the crops had been blessed, and some of the unchurched in the community had been prayed for.

In the years since, I have wondered how many things that I took for granted in that community were the result of those saints praying. What would it have looked like if they had not taken the privilege of prayer seriously? But can I be honest? Those prayer meetings were dull for me. I know I was a kid, but my memories of those meetings left me with a poor sense of the excitement in prayer. I'm grateful that the rest of the people in that church didn't let my lack of joy stop them from praying. Had they polled the junior department of the church, prayer meetings would have been replaced by ice cream socials, and as a result all of us kids might have been left to unblessed lives. So how did I learn to enjoy prayer? I'm still learning, but I do believe it is to be enjoyed, not just endured.

I wonder if everyone who has started writing a book on prayer feels the same. Surely there are plenty of options already on the shelves. And what do I know that others haven't already written much better? Wouldn't time be better spent praying than writing another book on the subject? P. T. Forsyth said, "No one ought to undertake it who has not spent more toil in the practice of prayer than on its principle."[1] If the only qualification to write on the subject is expertise, then I should save us all some time. If, on the other hand, the desire to encourage others to join in the greatest privilege on earth figures into the qualifications, I am eager to add my experience to yours in hopes that we all can touch the priceless treasure of partnering with our heavenly Father in the plan to bring His kingdom to earth.

With everything else that's going on in the world today, there is one thing that is obvious: God in His mercy has set His church to praying. Never in my lifetime have I seen so many people wanting to know about prayer and how it works. There are more prayer gatherings than since the great prayer revival of a prior century. In some countries where persecution has persisted, prayer has flourished for a long time. For instance, the Korean Christians who live in the tension of possible military invasion have been leaders in teaching all the church to pray. In Argentina, numerous reports of the burgeoning church credit prayer as the secret of its growth and effectiveness.

Missionaries report from diverse cultures in countries such as China, Israel, Iraq, the Philippines, and the Baltic republics that people are praying, both privately and in large public gatherings. Houses of prayer are forming on each city block in many parts of the United States. In almost unexplainable fashion, people from all nations are being alerted to pray.

Some are praying in desperation, some in a measure of increased faith, but without doubt, God is calling His people to pray. If what we have often heard is true—"When God gets ready to do something in the world, He sets His people to praying"—then something is up!

Why is there so much talk about prayer and so much guilt about not praying? I hardly ever meet a person who feels like he or she is good at prayer. Oh, some may refer to another's faithfulness in prayer or of their success in getting prayers answered, but when alone and honest the honorees confess to their sense of failure in prayer. What is the smoke screen that guards this most precious privilege? There are some misconceptions that trip up many on their way to the throne of grace.

Prayer as Currency

Sometimes we view the very act of prayer as a currency that can buy blessings from the great bank in the sky. It is as if God has something we want and we can get it if we put in enough phrases and hours of prayer. In this mindset, some issues cost more prayer than others. Since we don't always know the cost of each item, we are discouraged in our efforts until we have no other recourse than to *"pray it through."* If nothing seems to happen in answer, we conclude that we are too poor in prayer to gain anything from heaven.

I don't think heaven responds to our lobbying efforts. This same mentality can view prayer like a toll call where we vote for or against an issue. God is taking the calls and will favor the one who calls the most.

In my immaturity I faced this issue when I was playing football. I could never pray with much faith that our team would win. I knew the guys on the other side were lobbying for a win, too. Sometimes I thought, *If I can't outplay them, I'll out-pray them.* I should have practiced harder instead. God didn't respond to my lobbying attempts. Prayer is not an activity that can be used as currency to get stuff from the bank in heaven.

Duty

A second distraction from real prayer is the attitude that it is a duty. The dutiful pray-er says: "Prayer is one of the duties of a child of God. Fun or no fun, success or no success, I must pray. When I meet the judgment I will be asked how much I prayed. I must be able to give a good account of my praying activities." I would say that dutiful praying is better than no praying at all, but there is a higher level of prayer and we can enjoy it.

Discipline

The disciplinary pray-er says: "I am a godly person and godly people have certain disciplines in their lives. I must reveal to the world the superiority of the Christian lifestyle through my disciplines of Bible study, church attendance, tithing, prayer, and even the discipline of discipline. This makes me a good person."

There is great virtue in discipline when it is the result of an internalized value, but this view of prayer is pretty much joyless. It is hard to maintain discipline for the sake of being disciplined, whether it is in the area of exercising, eating, or praying. It is better than not praying, but again there is a higher level and we can know it.

Religious Activity

There has always been the tendency to view prayer as a religious activity for which we get badges of merit. "How long do you pray each day?" is a question often asked by young believers who want to gain some insight into the life of a successful saint. The picture here is of one who goes to a certain place, or takes a certain posture, or uses certain words. It is prayer as an event only.

One day as my family and I were driving together, my wife and I discussed prayer while the kids were busy in the backseat. My wife said, "You know, many of my prayers start with the word *and* because I try to keep a running conversation with the Father." Our daughter sat up excitedly and said, "You mean you can pray without first saying 'Dear God'?"

When prayer is an activity that takes place in a certain spot with a prescribed posture and in certain words, it makes us vulnerable to the guilt of neglect. Busyness and schedules take up the time we should spend doing the event. Then we feel less qualified to pray than ever. We are almost sure

God will not listen now because of our misplaced priorities. So we muddle into prayer with not much confidence that God cares or is willing to act on our behalf. What a trap.

I wish I could finally believe that prayer is as simple as Jesus says it is. Why do I seem intent on making it more complicated? Some time ago I was teaching a men's Bible study. One of the men who had recently committed his life to Christ said, "I have a question about prayer." I thought he was going to ask about how finite man could influence infinite God, or some other mystifying aspect of prayer. With manufactured confidence I responded, "Sure, what's your question?" "How does one address God?" he asked. "What do you say? 'Dear God'? You don't call Him 'mister,' do you?" I was both relieved and rebuked. The real obstacles to prayer aren't complicated. The complication comes from our misconceptions, not His requirements.

When prayer begins to take on a confusing agenda, I remember the story of Fifi and Charlie. Fifi was a little poodle with a pink bow tied neatly in her jeweled collar. Charlie was a bulldog with a rough and tough demeanor. They were discussing how one gets into the main house and how nice it was to be given that opportunity.

"I can get in anytime I want," said Fifi.

"No, you cannot!" growled Charlie. "I'm bigger than you and I can't get in. The handle is too high for either of us to reach and the door stays locked from the inside."

"I can get in," said Fifi.

"You're lying!" insisted Charlie. "How?"

Sheepishly, Fifi confided, "Well, I can't explain all the ins and outs of it. All I know is that when I scratch, the door opens."

Too simple? Maybe not.

Monologue Prayer

I was once involved in a situation with a man who made a corporate decision that affected me. He told me, "This is what we are going to do and I know it's right because I have prayed about it." My inner response was, *I'm not so sure because I have heard you pray.* Some of us think we have prayed when we have told God all the facts from our perspective and informed Him as to what will be taking place. He never is given a chance to get a word in edgewise. We work on our wording as if God is going to give a score on presentation. This may be good therapy, but it is very low-level praying. If prayer is anything of value, it is communication between us and God. If it is a one-way conversation, it is not communication.

I heard a communication expert say that people enjoy a meeting in direct proportion to their opportunity for input. I thought, *Maybe that's why God doesn't attend many of our religious meetings. He's never given the opportunity for input.* It could also be the reason He doesn't get as involved in our prayer sessions.

These are just some of the aberrations to real prayer. I really do not intend to mock these approaches to prayer. It *can* be a great event. It *can* happen in a certain place, with any given posture. But I am saying that prayer is more than this. There is a higher level of praying that glorifies

God and releases joy in the one praying. Why would we settle for low-level praying when high level is easier and more productive?

The Relationship of Prayer to Joy

In Jesus' last earthly discourse with His disciples, He revealed to them the very essence of life.[2] He tied together four great concepts: destiny, work, prayer, and joy. He explained to them that His *destiny* was to glorify the Father by revealing the Father's nature to those with whom he had influence *(work),* and that He did this by living in constant communion with the Father *(prayer).* This brought Him the greatest *joy* possible. The good news to the disciples and to us is that He gives us not only the model to follow but also the essence of life so we can live exactly the same way He does.

Here is the way it works: Jesus' highest joy came from revealing the nature of the Father to those who would submit to Him. He lived in constant communication with the Father and did everything in response to the Father's prompting. All the work, therefore, was originated by the Father and, having His nature stamped on it, brought glory to Him.

Now we are given the privilege to be the physical representations of Jesus on earth. Our destiny is to glorify God. We glorify Him by revealing His true nature to those who will listen. We reveal His nature by living in constant communication with Him and acting out of that relationship. When we see some area that needs the character of God infused into it, we pray and obey. He responds to our prayer and heaven moves into earth. He is glorified and we are flooded with joy in the privilege of being a part of the divine process.

> "I tell you the truth, anyone who has faith in me will do what I have been doing. He will do even greater things than these, because I am going to the Father. And I will do whatever you ask in my name, so that the Son may bring glory to the Father. You may ask me for anything in my name, and I will do it."[3]

Jesus said that the way to bring glory to the Father is to pray, knowing that God will be glorified through answering our prayers. It is through this process that the world gets to see the very nature of the Father.

Glorify is a verb that doesn't readily reveal a familiar action. How do you glorify? An old catechism asks, "What is the chief end of man?" Its answer includes, "To glorify God and enjoy him forever." That sounds great, but what exactly does it mean to glorify God? Jesus gave the complete answer:

> I have brought you glory on earth by completing the work you gave me to do.[4]

Then he described the work He was sent to do:

I have revealed you to those whom you gave me out of the world. They were yours; you gave them to me and they have obeyed your word.[5]

Just how do we apply this aspect of the model? Well, we have those who are under the umbrella of our influence. We are responsible to reveal the nature of God to them, just as Jesus was faithful in revealing the Father to those under His influence. But that is a big load to carry. How can we reveal the nature of God? Jesus did it this way: He listened to the Father and responded to Him (a good definition of prayer). The Father did the work and received the glory. Jesus was filled with joy in the relationship and enjoyed the fruit of His Father being revealed.

We can do that! We have all the equipment necessary to hear His voice and obey His words. Have you ever thought that one of the reasons we might have settled for mundane, joyless living is that we have not yet settled the issue that the purpose of our life is to glorify God? We certainly have good excuses to live selfishly. Our culture is centered on self-focus. It seems everyone is searching for "self." The great salvation that Jesus gives is liberation from the self-centered worldview. Wouldn't it be great to spend even one twenty-four-hour period without thinking about self? What a vacation! Jesus offers that vacation. Through His life, death, and resurrection He has saved us from the awful penalty of sin. He has defeated the god of this world and restored the authority of stewardship to the race of people established by Jesus, the last Adam. He has also made it possible for us to live beyond the narrow confines of life defined by "self."

I have a friend who has written a very good book entitled *I Was Always on My Mind*.[6] What a great title! That is our testimony, huh? We can't seem to escape the tyranny of morbid self-consciousness. The more we try to fix ourselves, the more entangled we become in the mire of thinking of self. There is true hope in the life Jesus gives us. He lived conscious of the Father. We can too.

> "In that day you will ask in my name. I am not saying that I will ask the Father on your behalf. No, the Father himself loves you because you have loved me and have believed that I came from God."[7]

It is a little difficult for us to believe that the Father loves us as much as He loves Jesus, and that He will be as responsive to our requests. But that is the way He describes this marvelous privilege we have in living in communion with God.

I think it would be fair to say that a one-word description for life properly aligned with God would be *joy*. To some this would be a self-serving motive for serving God. They would rather describe life in terms of duty, responsibility, self-denial, and obedience. These are all a part of the life, but without joy they misrepresent it.

> "Until now you have not asked for anything in my name. Ask and you will receive, and your joy will be made complete."[8]

"I am coming to you now, but I say these things while I am still in the world, so that they may have the full measure of my joy within them."9

If we take a close look at Jesus' life as the model for joy, we could conclude that joy at least looks like someone living with a consciousness of the real presence of God the Father. Added to that is a consciousness of actual union with the Father, and then a consciousness of the privilege of glorifying another. We will spend some time exploring how we can do this and what the obstacles are that often prevent us from getting it done. First we'll take a glimpse of prayer from a higher perspective. What does it look like from heaven?

CHAPTER TWO

INCENSE AND THUNDER

*J*esus made it clear that the key to His life and ministry was that He always looked into heaven to see what God was doing, and then He brought God's will into earth's atmosphere by faith. He instructed us to pray in the same way:

> "'Our Father in heaven, hallowed be your name, your kingdom come, your will be done on earth as it is in heaven.'"[1]

So we look into heaven, we see what the Father is doing, and then we bring it into earth through faith. When we look into heaven, what exactly do we see relating to prayer? In the book of Revelation, chapter 8, there is a picture of prayer.

The book of Revelation was an enigma to me for much of my Christian life. I would read Revelation and be confused by all the symbolism. Then one day, I just gazed at the title page and prayed. I said, "Lord, I don't understand this book, but I would like to because You promise a blessing to those who read it."[2] As I looked at the title, "The Revelation of Jesus Christ," it dawned on me that the book is not just about the last days—it's about Jesus Christ. The term *revelation* refers to information that is being transmitted beyond our natural ability to deduce or reason. So I began seeing the book as an opportunity to stick my head into heaven to see how things look in the heavenly realm.

In fact, I think that's exactly what the apostle John did when he was caught up in the Spirit. He was ushered by the Spirit into eternal time to see reality as it really is. He described what he saw in symbolic forms because it is very difficult to describe eternal realities that transcend time, language, and culture. Yet God showed him a beautiful picture of how things really look from heaven's perspective.

Incense, Fire, and Thunder

John saw a throne and Someone sitting on the throne. Around the throne were elders and four beasts who all worshiped God. The One sitting on the throne had a scroll in His hand sealed with seven seals. The Lion of the Tribe of Judah, appearing as a lamb who had been slain, came and took the scroll from the right hand of Him who sat on the throne:

And when he had taken it, the four living creatures and the twenty-four elders fell down before the Lamb. Each one had a harp and they were holding golden bowls full of incense, which are the prayers of the saints.[3]

Next John watched as the Lamb opened each of the seven seals, revealing the terrible judgments that will come upon the earth. Finally, John saw this scene:

> When he opened the seventh seal, there was silence in heaven for about half an hour. And I saw the seven angels who stand before God, and to them were given seven trumpets. Another angel, who had a golden censer, came and stood at the altar. He was given much incense to offer, with the prayers of all the saints, on the golden altar before the throne. The smoke of the incense, together with the prayers of all the saints, went up before God from the angel's hand. Then the angel took the censer, filled it with fire from the altar, and hurled it on the earth; and there came peals of thunder, rumblings, flashes of lightning and an earthquake.[4]

Here's the picture of what prayer looks like in heaven. It looks like incense going up before the altar of God. Every time we lift our hearts toward God in Jesus' name, an angel of God takes the incense in his hand (our prayers), mixes it with fire from the altar of God, flings it back to the earth, and it enters the earth's atmosphere as spiritual thunder, lightning, and earthquakes. That should give us some encouragement to pray! God has chosen to partner with us in transferring heaven into earth.

In case one might think I am way off base with this, we'll look at another passage and let Scripture comment on Scripture. David gives us a glimpse into the spiritual realm to reveal how the Lord answered his prayer:

> *In my distress I called to the LORD;*
> *I cried to my God for help.*
> *From his temple he heard my voice;*
> *my cry came before him, into his ears.*[5]

Notice the result:

> *The earth trembled and quaked,*
> *and the foundations of the mountains shook;*
> *they trembled because he was angry.*
> *Smoke rose from his nostrils;*
> *consuming fire came from his mouth,*
> *burning coals blazed out of it.*
> *He parted the heavens and came down;*
> *dark clouds were under his feet.*
> *He mounted the cherubim and flew;*
> *he soared on the wings of the wind.*
> *He made darkness his covering, his canopy around him—*
> *the dark rain clouds of the sky.*
> *Out of the brightness of his presence clouds advanced,*
> *with hailstones and bolts of lightning.*
> *The Lord thundered from heaven;*

the voice of the Most High resounded.
He shot his arrows and scattered the enemies,
great bolts of lightning and routed them.
The valleys of the sea were exposed
and the foundations of the earth laid bare
at your rebuke, O LORD,
at the blast of breath from your nostrils.
[Doesn't that sound like an earthquake?]
He reached down from on high and took hold of me;
he drew me out of deep waters.
He rescued me from my powerful enemy,
from my foes, who were too strong for me.
They confronted me in the day of my disaster,
but the LORD was my support.
He brought me out into a spacious place;
he rescued me because he delighted in me.[6] *(emphasis mine)*

That is what David saw in his spirit when he prayed. You might wonder if all those things literally happened. Did all that lightning and thunder and stuff happen physically and literally? I think David was giving us another glimpse into the heavenly realm of spiritual reality. In any case, God began to act. And when God acts, things on earth become subject to change. The ultimate result was that God delivered David from his distress. He delivered him from the enemies who had set a snare for him. He delivered him from the prison bars around him. As a result,

God's name was exalted and glorified in the life of this psalmist who prayed.

If we could only realize prayer is not wasted effort. Our prayers don't dissipate into the air, but instead are like incense going up before God, which is mixed with fire from His altar and flung back to earth in the form of thunder, lightning, and earthquakes. This truth should motivate us to discover in prayer the great privilege of working together with God to bring His will to pass on earth. When the world sees our prayers answered, they will see the kingdom of God expressed on the earth, and that will bring glory to the Father.

Perspective of the Early Church

One of the benefits of reading the book of Acts is that we get to see how the early church interpreted the teachings of Jesus. The question here is: Did the early church pray with this perspective? A quick overview of the book can give us some clues.

INVASION AT PENTECOST

When the Holy Spirit came in Acts, chapter 2, there was some obvious fire and thunder. The disciples gathered together to wait and pray for what Jesus had promised them. Suddenly, the Holy Spirit descended from heaven in a new way. There was the sound of violent wind blowing, and tongues of fire rested upon them. They began speaking in languages they didn't know, and about three thousand people witnessing this scene were converted into believers in Christ. That might be called an "earthquake." Then they started dwelling together as a community of believers.

> They devoted themselves to the apostles' teaching and to the fellowship, to the breaking of bread and to prayer.[7]

Notice the result this time.

> Everyone was filled with awe, and many wonders and miraculous signs were done by the apostles. All the believers were together and had everything in common.[8]

These believers had tapped into a cooperative prayer relationship with God...a real "co-op." They learned to live in union with Jesus Christ, the Father, and the Holy Spirit so that when they prayed, lightning, thunder, and earthquakes came from heaven to shake things up on the earth.

PETER, JOHN, AND A CRIPPLED MAN

In the third chapter of Acts, we learn that Peter and John were on their way to the temple one day and they came across a crippled man asking for alms. Peter and John told the man they didn't have money to give him, but they had something better. After Peter commanded the man to walk in the name of Jesus Christ, great controversy erupted among the religious leaders. They called Peter and John in to question them and told them to quit preaching in Jesus' name. After they were released, the believers gathered together to pray.

> They raised their voices together in prayer to God. "Sovereign Lord," they said, "you made the heaven and the earth and the sea, and everything in them. You spoke by the Holy Spirit through the mouth of your servant, our father David: 'Why do the nations rage and the peoples plot in vain? The kings of the earth take their stand and the rulers gather together against the Lord and against his Anointed One.'"9

Notice what they were saying. They said, "Lord, we're just a little band of disciples. The Roman government with all its influence and the Jewish religious system with all its manipulative power and evil spirits are against us. But God, we're talking to *You*. You are the sovereign God who has already taken into consideration this whole thing, and we believe you can provide an earthquake, some thunder, or lightning" (my paraphrase). So they continued to pray.

> After they prayed, the place where they were meeting was shaken. And they were all filled with the Holy Spirit and spoke the word of God boldly.10

This boldness and power of the Spirit resulted in all kinds of miracles done in their midst. The church prayed, incense went up before the

Father, and thunder and lightning came down. As a result, their situation on earth was heavily impacted by the shaking power of God.

PHILIP AND STEPHEN

By the sixth chapter of Acts, things were getting busy for the apostles. They were getting spread too thin trying to take care of everyone's needs, so they decided to pick some godly men to help them. The apostles chose Philip and Stephen, among others, to take care of the ministry of helps and administration so they could give their attention to prayer and to the ministry of the Word. Note the result of their commitment to prayer.

So the word of God spread. The number of disciples in Jerusalem increased rapidly, and a large number of priests became obedient to the faith.[11]

The ministry of Stephen and Philip manifested in miraculous power. Philip went down to Samaria and preached about Jesus. Philip was not an apostle, but a deacon who preached a simple message about Jesus and the kingdom of God, and great miracles resulted. Philip was transported down into Egypt, and the Ethiopian eunuch was converted (thunder, lightning, earthquake). Why? Because when the apostles made a priority of prayer and the ministry of the Word, they saw thunder and lightning from heaven displayed through this common man. Stephen, another non-apostle filled with the Holy Spirit, did great wonders and miraculous signs. He preached one of the greatest sermons ever preached to the

Jewish leaders, after which he was stoned and taken gloriously up to heaven (thunder, rumblings).

The lightning occurred at the conversion of Saul, who had witnessed Stephen's death. Saul was persecuting the church, killing Christians, throwing them in jail, and so the church prayed. I don't know exactly what they were praying, but had I been one of them, I'd have prayed, "Oh God, eliminate Saul! Come on, God, get rid of him, stop him." I don't know exactly what their prayer was, but that incense went through the heavenlies; then the angel of the Lord grabbed those prayers of the saints for Saul, mixed them with God's fire, and slung them back to the earth. Saul was struck by holy lightning on his way back to Damascus.

> As he neared Damascus on his journey, suddenly a light from heaven flashed around him. He fell to the ground and heard a voice say to him, "Saul, Saul, why do you persecute me?"
>
> "Who are you, Lord?" Saul asked.
>
> "I am Jesus, whom you are persecuting," he replied. "Now get up and go into the city, and you will be told what you must do."[12]

That flash of light brought life to Paul's spirit. Saul the Persecutor was changed to Paul the Apostle, the great missionary and preacher. What a lightning strike, what an earthquake, what thunder! It all happened as God's people were in prayer and God acted.

CORNELIUS THE GENTILE

Then we come to the story of Cornelius, the Gentile, in the tenth chapter of Acts. He didn't have any covenant rights, as defined by Jewish law; however, the Bible describes him as God-fearing, devout, and a man of prayer. One afternoon an angel of God appeared to Cornelius to let him know what his prayers had accomplished:

> Your prayers and gifts to the poor have come up as a memorial offering before God. Now send men to Joppa to bring back a man named Simon who is called Peter.[13]

Meanwhile, God showed Peter in a vision that he should not call any man impure or unclean. Just then Cornelius's servants arrived, and Peter went back with them to Cornelius's house. After Peter shared the gospel with Cornelius and his Gentile friends, they were converted and filled with the Spirit. What began in prayer with Cornelius culminated in a major spiritual earthquake for the entire body of Christ. The wall of division between Jew and Gentile was pulled down by the power of God that day at Cornelius's house.

We could stand that kind of earthquake today to break down the walls between races, between classes, and to obliterate the sectarianism that separates the body of Christ. If God pulled down the wall between Jew and Gentile, which is the strongest wall ever to exist between two groups of people, then God can do the same in our country and in our world.

PETER IN PRISON AND
KING HEROD WITH WORMS

Another powerful instance of answered prayer occurred when King
Herod tried to get rid of Peter by putting him into prison.

> So Peter was kept in prison, but the church was earnestly pray-
> ing to God for him.[14]

More incense went up to heaven on behalf of Peter. That incense was
mixed with fire from the altar, flung back to earth, and here is what happened: An angel appeared to Peter in prison and walked him out of the
prison into the street. It was such a mysterious event for Peter, he didn't
know if he was dreaming or if it was reality. As he began to see familiar
landmarks, he thought, *Man, this must be real.* So he went to the house
where the believers were praying for him.

> Peter knocked at the outer entrance, and a servant girl named
> Rhoda came to answer the door. When she recognized Peter's
> voice, she was so overjoyed she ran back without opening it and
> exclaimed, "Peter is at the door!"
>
> "You're out of your mind," they told her. When she kept
> insisting that it was so, they said, "It must be his angel."
>
> But Peter kept on knocking, and when they opened the door
> and saw him, they were astonished.[15]

What was the fate of Herod?

Because Herod did not give praise to God, an angel of the Lord struck him down [lightning], and he was eaten by worms and died.
But the word of God continued to increase and spread.[16]

God heard the prayers of His people and expressed His glory by delivering Peter from jail. In addition to that, the very man who had tried to stop the gospel from spreading was struck by heavenly lightning in his tracks.

PAUL AND BARNABAS SENT OFF WITH POWER

There was more incense being kindled in prayer by the believers in Antioch.

While they were worshiping the Lord and fasting, the Holy Spirit said, "Set apart for me Barnabas and Saul for the work to which I have called them." So after they had fasted and prayed, they placed their hands on them and sent them off.[17]

Paul and Barnabas were sent off on their great missionary endeavor with much incense going up to heaven. This resulted in many miraculous events. The word of God was preached in power to many nations (thunder), and the truth of the gospel was revealed as never before (lightning). Everywhere they traveled there was a shaking of events (earthquakes), causing the lightning and thunder to be received.

We need some earthshaking miracles, but we must realize that when God starts shaking things up, there is going to be controversy. There is going to be controversy with governments at every level, with religious denominations, and throughout our social structure. In the midst of the shaking there will be thunder—the voice of God coming forth to proclaim truth—and lightning—God revealing things to people beyond their ability to reason. There will be no real change without these. We're not going to change things by adapting to the world system. We can by superimposing the kingdom of God over the system that's in existence.

PAUL AND SILAS IN AN EARTHQUAKE

Paul and Silas provide our next example of answered prayer. They delivered a slave girl from a demonic spirit, which enabled her to predict the future. Her owners became upset when they realized their "prophet" could no longer be used for profit, so they had Paul and Silas put in jail. But a dramatic turn of events was recorded.

> About midnight Paul and Silas were praying and singing hymns to God....Suddenly there was such a violent earthquake that the foundations of the prison were shaken. At once all the prison doors flew open, and everybody's chains came loose.[18]

You know the story. The jailer started to kill himself, but was saved instead when Paul and Silas ministered the gospel to him and his family. In this instance, an actual earthquake did take place. But the most impressive earthquake wasn't the one that opened the prison doors; it was the one that opened the door to the jailer's heart, and to the gospel in that whole area. A little incense went up toward heaven, and thunder, lightning, and an earthquake came back down, bringing the kingdom of God to earth out of heaven.

PAUL IN TYRE AND RIOT IN JERUSALEM

A brief passage in chapter 21 might be overlooked as just a footnote to Paul's travel schedule. It describes what occurred when Paul left Tyre.

> But when our time was up, we left and continued on our way. All the disciples and their wives and children accompanied us out of the city, and there on the beach we knelt to pray. After saying good-by to each other, we went aboard the ship, and they returned home.[19]

The significant thing about this is that the next phase of Paul's journey took him to Jerusalem, where perhaps the greatest controversy or "earthquake" in Paul's whole life happened. When he preached the gospel in Jerusalem, he was accused of being against his own people, the law, and the temple; he was arrested there and finally wound up in Rome. The earthquakes, thunder, and lightning that occurred in Jerusalem might be attributed to that little prayer meeting on the beach in Tyre. The believers sent a little incense up to heaven, God mixed it with fire from the altar, flung it down, and, following an attempted

lynching, Paul had the opportunity to preach the gospel to Jewish leaders and Roman governors.

PAUL IN SHIPWRECK AND BITTEN BY SNAKE

In Acts 27, we find that Paul was being transported as a prisoner on
board a ship sailing for Rome. Paul tried to warn the sailors not to leave
port, but they didn't listen and were caught in a hurricane. Paul encouraged the desperate crew:

> "But now I urge you to keep up your courage, because not one
> of you will be lost; only the ship will be destroyed. Last night an
> angel of the God whose I am and whom I serve stood beside me
> and said, 'Do not be afraid, Paul. You must stand trial before
> Caesar; and God has graciously given you the lives of all who sail
> with you.' So keep up your courage, men, for I have faith in God
> that it will happen just as He told me. Nevertheless, we must run
> aground on some island."[20]

It is as if Paul was telling them, "Cheer up, I saw a little lightning last
night. The angel of God appeared to me, and everybody's going to be
okay." Miraculously, not a soul was lost. They made it to the island of
Malta, where they were welcomed by the natives. As Paul was stoking the
fire, a snake fastened itself to his hand, and the natives thought it was a
sign that he was a murderer. But when Paul, unharmed, shook the snake
off into the fire, they thought he was a god. Next, Paul prayed for the sick

father of the chief official of Malta, and the man was healed. This caused the rest of the sick people on the island to come and be cured. As a result, the glory of God was expressed to these people who had no concept of what God was really like. And so the rumblings of God's holy thunder were felt on the island of Malta. Finally, Paul went on to Rome. The book of Acts ends with this statement about him:

> Boldly and without hindrance he preached the kingdom of God and taught about the Lord Jesus Christ.[21]

Those examples should help us see what God's thunder, lightning, and earthquakes look like when they come back to the earth!

Participating in God's Co-Op

The message here is that we should not be discouraged when we encounter problems in our lives, because we have the privilege of participating in a prayer "co-op" with God. We can be His representatives on the earth. The big question is: How do we do it? Here are four suggestions.

GOD'S WILL

First of all, it is imperative to believe this is God's will. Our big problem is we have trouble believing that we enjoy the same privilege and responsibility that Jesus does with the Father. We doubt what Jesus said in John, chapters 14 through 17:

"I came to glorify the Father and here is how I did it: I would hear the Father speak, I would pray, and the Father would answer from heaven and express His glory. The Holy Spirit is going to come. It is imperative that I go away so He can come and live in you. In that day you will recognize that I am in the Father, and that you are in Me so you are in the Father. You are going to have the same responsibility I had on earth to pray and see God move heaven into earth." (my paraphrase)

I want to examine several verses in order to help us all to believe.

"On that day you will realize that I am in my Father, and you are in me, and I am in you. Whoever has my commands and obeys them, he is the one who loves me. He who loves me will be loved by my Father, and I too will love him and show myself to him."[22]

Here is a pertinent question: What made it possible for Jesus to live His whole life on earth for the sole purpose of expressing the nature of the Father? The answer: He was aware that He was loved by the Father. The devil has tried to convince us in every way that we are not unconditionally loved by God; that we are not good enough, forgiven enough, or mature enough. Because we are in Christ, we receive the same love from the Father that Christ receives. The Father loves the Son completely, without measure, unconditionally, eternally, with His whole heart. We are loved the same. One of the Father's expressions of love to us is that

He will hear our prayer and send lightning, thunder, and earthquakes back to the earth.

Jesus continued to explain in the following passage that one of the major expressions of the love of the Father for us is His desire to answer our prayer.

"If you remain in me and my words remain in you, ask whatever you wish, and it will be given you. This is to my Father's glory, that you bear much fruit, showing yourselves to be my disciples."[23]

You might think, "But it says I've got to remain in Him and His words must remain in me." Yet the next verse tells you how simple it is:

"As the Father has loved me, so have I loved you. Now remain in my love."[24]

I remain by just continuing to be loved by Jesus. You raise the objection, *"But I'm not perfect."* That's not the issue; are you loved?

In fact, we have no option to be perfect (without sin). We have already forfeited that. Now our only choice is to receive His love or reject it. Jesus clarified it for us:

"If you obey my commands, you will remain in my love, just as I have obeyed my Father's commands and remain in his love."[25]

"You did not choose me, but I chose you and appointed you to go and bear fruit—fruit that will last. Then the Father will give you whatever you ask in my name. This is my command: Love each other."[26]

Is the picture becoming clearer? The love of the Father is expressed to us as He delights in listening to our requests and answering them by shaking things up down here.

So we must believe that it is God's will for us to represent Him on earth. As we receive His love, we can ask as confident children and believe that God has placed us in the same position Jesus was in while on earth—seeing what needs to be changed and praying that the kingdom of God will be done on earth as it is in heaven.

GLORIFY THE FATHER

The second way to represent Him is to accept that our purpose on earth is to glorify the Father. The purpose is not to have a comfortable life, or a successful business or ministry. The highest purpose on the earth is to glorify the Father. Without adopting that purpose, prayer will never be meaningful. But if our single purpose on the earth is to glorify the Father, then we're going to be able to hear God's instructions clearly. He will give His instructions to the one who is determined to fulfill the eternal purpose.

ACCEPT RESPONSIBILITY OVER OUR REALMS

The third way to represent the Father is to accept responsibility over the particular realms He has given us: body, mind, friends, family, and whatever influence we have. We must have the courage to pray, "Okay, God, I need your earthquakes, lightning, or thunder in my spheres of responsibility. I need your word to thunder forth in the proclamation of truth. I need the revelatory lightning from heaven. I need the earthquakes of your shaking something up." No timidity. There's a lot at stake: family, church, city, state, nation—even a world!

We ought to pray about everything that concerns us. If you want to pray for a parking place, fine. But please! Let's not confine our prayers to parking places! Let's pray that God will break down the walls that divide races, denominations, social classes, and the children of God—let's pray for an *earthquake!* Let's pray for our loved ones who are away from God—let's pray that the *thunder* of the word of God will displace the noise of demonic deception! Let's pray that the *lightning* of revelation of the resurrected Christ will strike our loved ones as it did Paul on the road to Damascus. We may know people imprisoned by drugs, pornography, sexual perversion, or occult deception. Hey! Peter was in prison, the church prayed, and he was set free. Let's pray that God will open some prison doors. Let's accept our responsibility over our realm.

ENGAGE

The fourth way to represent God is to engage. God wants to magnify the name of Jesus. When Jesus was praying for us, He gave us great insight into what was happening to Him and His disciples:

"I will remain in the world no longer, but they are still in the world, and I am coming to you. Holy Father, protect them by the power of your name—the name you gave me—so that they may be one as we are one. While I was with them, I protected them and kept them safe by that name you gave me."[27]

The ability of Jesus to protect the disciples was in the authority of the name He was given. We have been given authority through the name of Jesus. When we start learning to use that authority we can implement some protection by bringing heaven's authority to earth.

"All the nations surrounded me, but in the name of the LORD I cut them off.[28]

I know there are a lot of demons in hell and I know they have a lot of influence in the political and in the religious realms. But when the nations surround us, we can cut them off in the name of Jesus:

They surrounded me on every side, but in the name of the LORD I cut them off. They swarmed around me like bees, but they died out as quickly as burning thorns; in the name of the LORD I cut them off. I was pushed back and about to fall, but the LORD helped me. The LORD is my strength and my song; he has become my salvation."[29]

The name of the Lord is strong. When we start using it, we will start to see some things happen. Engage!

You might think, "How do I engage?" As we accept responsibility over situations, we listen quietly. We listen for a long time, if necessary. What does God want us to pray? Sometimes we pray too quickly: "Oh God, fix this, fix this." Let's try more listening. However, we can't wait forever to be sure. At some point, we just start praying.

I don't think the early church prayed concerning Saul, "Lord, let him go out and see Stephen get stoned, then when he's on his way to Damascus strike him down and speak to him." I don't think they had that much detail in mind. I think they were praying to a sovereign God who they believed could handle the situation any way He chose. They might have prayed, "Oh Lord, here's a man who is killing the believers. God, he needs to be shaken (earthquake)! He needs thunder! He needs lightning!" Whatever they said, God answered it His way. He mixed the prayers of the saints with the fire from His altar.

In other words, God has the final say-so in how He answers. He doesn't just take our orders and fulfill them without adding His will. He takes our incense, interprets it, mixes it with His fire, His timetable, His agenda, His purposes, and then He slings it back to the earth. But He does answer. It will be according to His calendar and His agenda, but it will be done to glorify His name. And that is fine with us. That's our purpose, too!

Pray expectantly. Expect God to answer. What if He doesn't? Then we might get disappointed. But let's not allow our fear of disappointment to keep us from expecting God to move. If we are expecting God to glorify His name, we won't be disappointed. If we are expecting God to live by our dictates, we will be disappointed. But God is looking for ways to show His love toward us. He wants to show His love by sending thunder, lightning, and earthquakes back to earth in answer to our prayers.

So let's smoke up heaven. Let's begin sending up our incense. Let's keep the angels of God busy taking that incense, mixing it with fire from the altar, and slinging it back to the earth—and we will see the glory of God manifested on the earth.

> *Father, I know You are stirring people to pray. I pray that this chapter will encourage people to get serious about praying. Some are living in hopelessness right now because of some terrible circumstances in their lives. Let them see, Lord, there is nothing that your thunder, lightning, or earthquake couldn't affect. Let us believe that heaven rules over earth, and that the name of Jesus is stronger than every other name. Give us faith to believe in your miracles, signs, wonders, healing, and salvation. We need your word to come forth in boldness like thunder, your revelation to hit like lightning, and your earthquakes to shake impossible situations. Father, give us the faith to believe in Jesus' name. Amen.*

CHAPTER THREE

OBSTACLES TO JOYFUL PRAYING

Since we are created in the image of God and for His glory, we know that we are made for intimacy and impact. Dr. Larry Crabb has written extensively to help us see that all humanity has the deep longing to be loved unconditionally and to feel that our existence makes some eternal impact.[1] The life of joyful prayer fulfills both of these basic desires. Jesus has taken our place in separation from the Father so that we can have His place in the eternal presence of the Father. God has also given us the dignity to represent Him on earth just as Jesus did while in the physical body. The normal life of a regenerated believer is to live conscious of God's presence while exercising heaven's authority on earth:

> "I tell you the truth, anyone who has faith in me will do what I have been doing. He will do even greater things than these, because I am going to the Father. And I will do whatever you ask in my name, so that the Son may bring glory to the Father. You may ask me for anything in my name, and I will do it."[2]

If this is so simple, why is it so hard to live out? Well, there are some obstacles. And that brings up another question. Why does God allow obstacles to deter us from being what He designed us to be? Let's take a look at this.

Obstacles for Growth

God's kingdom includes growth as an integral part of His design. For instance, He created Adam and Eve in purity and innocence, but they had potential for growth. They were created in the image of God, with the command to subdue the earth. They were given the corresponding abilities to accomplish this commission. In short, they had the potential and privilege to grow through facing the challenges of their work.

Another illustration of this principle is found in the Old Testament story of God leaving enemy armies in the land on purpose.

> These are the nations the LORD left to test all those Israelites who had not experienced any of the wars in Canaan (he did this only to teach warfare to the descendants of the Israelites who had not had previous battle experience).[3]

So, an obvious question arises: What do I need to learn from war other than to avoid it? Since God is interested in our being His physical representatives on earth, He wants us to reveal His victory over all the enemies of His kingdom. Or to add another slant, we won't discover our full authority and power until the critical need requires it. It is in war that we are pressed to the end of ourselves and into His strength. In the face of a superior force, we are forced to discover the ultimate force—the name of Jesus.

"You may ask me for anything in my name, and I will do it."[4]

Periodically, I hear someone say (not often in the United States): "I don't understand football. Why all the fuss and interest?" Well, football is not a complicated game to understand. Eleven men are to devise a way to get the ball across the goal line. I attended college on a scholarship to play football. We reported in mid-August to begin practice for the upcoming season. There were hours given to getting in physical condition and even more hours given to strategy. We had intricate plays designed to run and pass the ball over the goal line. It is important to not only know what to do and be physically able to do it, but the timing has to be right or the eleven men will stumble over each other and not get the job done.

Now the most intriguing thing happened near the first week in September. We traveled hundreds of miles to meet someone whose intent was to stop us from advancing the ball across the goal line. This is confusing, huh? All that money for scholarships, all the time, all the sweat to get that ball over the goal line, and now we are looking for someone to stop us. Maybe this game is more complicated than I thought. Another twist to this saga is that we enjoyed the games when the opposition was so good that it was difficult to get our job done. We relished the close wins.

We discovered that the big obstacles drew the best out of us. The best in the believer is a faith that draws on the life of Jesus who lives in us. Let's look at some of the most common obstacles.

The Counterfeit of Self-Righteousness

The most common obstacle to any real achievement in life is the counterfeit. It seems that the devil has left no stone unturned to produce a perfected counterfeit to distract real believers from the normal life of intimacy and impact. This counterfeit can be described in one word: self-righteousness. Some of the major players in the New Testament drama are the religious leaders who provided Jesus' greatest obstacle to expressing the Father's life in the world. The Pharisees and Sadducees were sure their righteousness was superior to all others'. These religious leaders were the human manifestations of self-righteousness. Self-righteousness is the belief that anything I do gains me favor with God. Inherent in that definition is the idea that for people to be self-righteous, they have to undervalue their own depravity as well as the grace of God.

JACOB'S LADDER

One of my early mentors in ministry was Roy Hession. I have never met anyone on earth who better understood the nature of the grace of God than Roy Hession. One of his favorite stories was the tale of Jacob's ladder. He would relish making the connection between Jacob's ladder and the ladders that all of us try to build. He said that all of us use religious ladders to try to get from where we are into the presence of God.

These ladders have some common characteristics. First, they never start where we are. All our ladders seem to start one rung above our reach. We often say things such as, "If I could pray more…" or "If I were a more diligent student…" or "If I had more discipline…" or "If I could only get over my besetting sin, etc., then I know I would enjoy the presence of God." The problem with all our ladders is that they never start where we are.

Secondly, our ladders never reach all the way to heaven. They give us some sense of superiority because they reach higher than we were before, but if we should achieve our goal of climbing our particular ladder, we find that at the top there is a condescending attitude toward those who haven't climbed as far.

I often hear this reflected in testimonies such as, "I can remember a time when I had trouble getting up early in the morning to spend time with God, but I have no trouble with that now," or "I can remember a time when it was hard for me to forgive, but now I don't," with the implication being that those who have not yet climbed the ladder are, in some way, inferior.

Another characteristic of our ladders is that they all require climbing, and none of us have the strength to climb into the presence of God. So again, it is a misconception of where we are, what abilities we have, and what it means to live in the grace of God.

That which replaces good works of righteous living is often the dead works of religious striving. Anything that we do on our own initiative to make ourselves more acceptable to God—whether it be an act of self-denial or a religious activity—is nothing more than a dead work. Dead works clog up our lives so that we are unable to truly communicate with God and exhibit the expressions of His righteous works through us. I think that our archenemy, the devil, would rather have our lives cluttered with dead works than to have us involved in wicked works. If we commit wicked works, we will be convicted and drawn to repentance. Dead works give some solace to the guilty soul. Dead works are the perfect counterfeit and obstacle to the life of peace and power.

THE SYMPTOM OF BLINDNESS

With much of the focus in the New Testament on Jesus' encounters with counterfeit life, we discover some tools to detect this major obstacle. Maybe the most hideous symptom of self-righteousness is the blindness that accompanies it. If they weren't so self-indicting, the stories of the New Testament would actually be a comedy as we see the Pharisees totally missing what Jesus was really talking about.

One of the most comedic chapters in the whole Bible is in John's Gospel, chapter 9. It is the story of Jesus healing the man who was blind from birth. We really don't know much about this man until his encounter with Jesus. We'll call him Ralph since we're pretty sure this was not his name. Ralph was old enough to be recognized as an adult, yet he was young enough to still be under the supervision of his parents, so we'll assume that Ralph was approximately nineteen. Here we have this nineteen-year-old who has never seen the light of day, the bloom of a flower, or the smile of a child. One day Jesus comes by, takes spittle and dirt, mixes it together, places it in Ralph's eye sockets, and tells him to go across town and wash his eyes.

Everything Jesus did taught something about the reality of the life he was demonstrating. I believe He intended to show those who were watching that to be cleansed of blindness, we must be willing to submit even to that which we do not understand, and which might be even humiliating. It doesn't make any sense to add to a man's blindness by putting dirt into his eyes. Maybe Jesus was saying to those Pharisees who were watching: "If you guys want to be free from your blindness, you must be willing for God to humble your rigid reason and your right dogma in order to experience His life."

Anyway, here goes Ralph across town. I'm sure there were people who saw the mud trickling down his face and asked where he was going. It had to be somewhat humbling for him to say, "I'm going to get my sight." They would certainly not have understood; he would have been not only blind, but also the object of ridicule from his friends. However, when he got to the pool to which he was sent, he washed his eyes. Not only did the mud come out—the blindness was washed away, too.

Yet when Ralph got back home, instead of people rejoicing over this miracle healing, there was great consternation. An argument broke out over whether or not this was Ralph. Some believed that he was an imposter. They would rather have believed that a trick had been played on them than that a common Nazarene could have performed such a miracle. Finally, Ralph spoke up and said in effect, "If it matters, I am

Ralph. I am the guy that you've known my whole life." But they still weren't satisfied. They wanted the opinion of the religious leaders, so they sent for the Pharisees. The Pharisees came and began to question both Ralph and his parents. Ralph was adamant that he didn't know much theology and dogma, but he was sure of one thing: his eyes had been healed. His parents realized that they were caught in a dilemma—if they confessed the truth about Jesus, they risked getting kicked out of the synagogue and Jewish social life. They chose to cling to their religious and social connections and ignore all that they knew about their son's dramatic healing.

In the midst of the inquisition, the Pharisees said a very revealing thing. They denounced Ralph for his lack of qualifications theologically, saying openly and proudly, "We are Moses' disciples," not knowing that they had just exposed their major problem. They chose to let Moses be the final revelation of the nature of God when, in fact, he was only a part.

In the past God spoke to our forefathers through the prophets at many times and in various ways, but in these last days he has spoken to us by his Son, whom he appointed heir of all things, and through whom he made the universe. The Son is the radiance of God's glory and the exact representation of his being, sustaining all things by his powerful word. After he had provided purification for sins, he sat down at the right hand of the Majesty in heaven.[5]

Because they had chosen Moses to be their final revelation of God, the Pharisees were unable to recognize the very Word of God when He came on the scene. This was the key to their blindness. What a tragedy. They lived in the midst of the Living Word of God, yet they spent all their time digging through the minutia of Scripture trying to find the very truth that was walking among them in fullness.

We could laugh at the Pharisees if it weren't that all of us carry some of that self-righteous blindness in us. It is only by God's mercy that we are not totally blind as the Pharisees. Make no mistake about it. Self-righteousness did not die with the Pharisees. It is still around in all men and women who have trouble recognizing that their only right in the presence of God is by grace through faith. There is nothing that we can do to make ourselves more acceptable to God. But we *are* accepted on the basis of Jesus' life, death, burial, resurrection, and ascension for us. If we believe that, then we can live in the constant presence of God. If we refuse to believe that, nothing we can do will make us more acceptable.

Roy Hession would close his message on Jacob's ladder by pointing out that the ladder represented Jesus. Jacob's ladder was an Old Testament representation of the Jesus who would come. The ladder that Jacob dreamed of that night started right where he was, reached all the way to the presence of God, and did not require climbing. Jacob saw angels ascending and descending on the ladder. The angels from below were ascending to heaven to report the need of the one who was lying helpless on earth. The angels descending were bringing down specific provisions for the needy sinner.

This is a beautiful picture of the grace revealed in Jesus Christ. He comes to where we are in our sin and condemnation and makes it possible for us to enjoy the very essence of God. He descended into our sin, won the battle against sin and Satan, and then ascended to heaven to make it possible for us to live in the constant and conscious presence of God Himself.

CONTEMPT OF OTHERS

There are some other clues in the New Testament to help us detect the presence of this hideous obstacle of self-righteousness. One of the most embarrassing symptoms is found in Luke 18:9–14. This is the story of the sinner and the Pharisee. Jesus told this story to expose the subtle, self-righteous contempt in the Pharisee. Exposure is complete when the Pharisee says, "God, I thank you that I am not like other men—robbers, evildoers, adulterers—or even like this tax collector."[6]

Any attitude of contempt for others who don't live by our standard of righteousness is a sure sign of self-righteousness. Have you noticed how easy it is to come up with your own standard that you declare is pleasing to God? I personally grew up in a tradition where if we went to church and tithed and read our Bibles periodically, and didn't smoke, drink, and dance, we were considered righteous. It was not emphasized that we should live with mercy, and the issue of racial prejudice was hardly ever mentioned. It was fairly simple to stand smugly righteous in church while others were considered in some way inferior because of the color of their skin or their educational or social background or their non-church-attending behavior.

In some traditions the standard of righteousness includes the clothes you wear, the length of your hair, or the places you go for entertainment. In other places it includes your style of worship. There just seems to be no end to our creativity in defining righteousness in terms of those things that we do and others don't.

The operative word here, however, is the *contempt* we have. It is obvious that by God's design we all grew up in different cultures. Not all of us will do things the same way, nor are cultural norms constant throughout the world. To recognize these differences and even to struggle with them is not the issue here. The issue is the attitude of contempt or feelings of superiority that we have because others do not live up to our definitions of righteousness.

On another occasion Jesus told a story to expose a different form of blindness. A religious lawyer had asked Jesus what he should do to inherit eternal life. Since the lawyer wanted to focus on what a man can *do,* Jesus asked him how he interpreted the law. The man responded with the correct answer:

"'Love the Lord your God with all your heart and with all your soul and with all your strength and with all your mind'; and, 'Love your neighbor as yourself.'"[7]

Jesus slapped self-righteousness squarely in the face when He told the lawyer it's not enough to know the answer; you have to do it.

"You have answered correctly. Do this and you will live."[8]

The lawyer felt so intimidated by Jesus' answer that he sought to justify himself by asking,

"And who is my neighbor?"[9]

This aspect of self-righteousness is one of the most damning. It was something that had strangled the Jewish people for years. They incorrectly believed that because they had been given the law, possession of the law made them righteous. They looked down their spiritual noses at the Gentiles, who had not been chosen by God to be the recipients of His law.

But this is not a mistake made only by the Old Testament Jews or the New Testament Pharisees. It is a mistake that is often made today. We tend to think that because we know something, we possess it. Jesus said it is not possessed until it is practiced. Jesus illustrated this as He both proclaimed the presence of the kingdom of God and practiced it. He forgave sin, healed the sick, cast out demons, and raised the dead. He gave His disciples the commission to do the same.[10]

To preach the present reign of God without demonstrating it is to preach an incomplete gospel. Some have gone to great lengths seeking to prove that the reign of God is delayed until the future. They are left with a gospel of propositions for the mind, devoid of the power of a present kingdom.

The lawyer made an A on his biblical knowledge but earned an F in the lesson of life. Jesus went on to expose this self-righteousness even more as He told about religious people (the priests and the Levites) who were so busy with their religious activities that they had no time for a man who had been beaten and left in a ditch on the way to Jericho.[11] The star of the story was a Samaritan who, though he was a despised individual, practiced the fulfillment of what the lawyer had answered. Samaritans were considered by the Jews to be the scum of the earth. They were half-breeds and theological heretics. Even Jesus Himself, in His encounter with the woman at the well, indicated that the Samaritans were wrong in some aspects of their theology. So here we have it: a half-breed, socially inept, theologically incorrect man who is practicing the essence of God's law, while the lawyer, who is a member of the Jewish race and has been privileged to know the law of God, is blinded by his own self-righteousness.

We can begin to see how self-righteousness presents a major obstacle in the life of those who want to live in constant communion with God.

PASSION OR DOGMA AND DUTY?

Another devastating aspect of self-righteousness is that it reduces to dogma and duty a life that was designed to be lived only in passion. This is illustrated in the story of Jesus having dinner with a particular Pharisee.[12] During dinner a prostitute comes in off the street and begins to show affection to Him by washing His feet and kissing them. The Pharisees are appalled by this action. They accuse Jesus of being non-discerning in that He does not rebuke this woman. He reveals that He is more than discerning as He reads their minds and hearts and tells them what they were thinking. In His mercy He exposes this passionless blindness in the Pharisees by telling them a little story and asking them a question.

The story goes sort of like this: There were two men who owed debts to a common creditor. One owed the equivalent of one thousand dollars and one owed the equivalent of ten dollars. The creditor forgave them both. Which one would love him the most? Again, the Pharisees show their mental acumen by answering correctly that the one who had been given the most would love the most. Jesus then lifts the curtain from their obvious blindness. He has been in their presence for hours and no one has responded to Him with any kind of passion, affection, or appreciation. This woman came in and immediately began showing Him lavish and passionate affection. The difference, says Jesus, is that she is conscious that she has been forgiven much, while those sitting around the table are not aware that they even need forgiveness. So, in this climactic story, Jesus connects our sense of forgiveness with our passionate love.

Those who have chosen to live the Christian life in terms of dogma and duty have missed the point altogether. None of us has escaped the ravages of sin on the human race and in our personal lives. To live unconscious of our constant need of God's mercy and without a constant appreciation for His forgiveness is to live in a spiritual arrogance that invites destruction.

Maybe one of the reasons our current brand of Christianity is so hard to export on the mission field is that it is a poor substitute for passionate living. I am convinced that new generations are going to follow that religion that offers them a chance to live passionately. There never has been, nor ever shall be, a better reason to live passionately than to know the God of the Bible who, in His immeasurable love, sent His own Son to die in our place so that we could be forgiven of all of our sins—past, present, and future—and live in His constant presence, representing Him in a world and carrying out His government as He gives daily directions.

PERVERTED CONSCIOUSNESS

One of the funny scenes Jesus described in His Sermon on the Mount was a picture of Pharisees standing on the street corners praying loudly so that others around would know they were praying.[13] I can see it now, the Pharisee going out early in the morning and looking for the most crowded street corner. He will only begin his prayer when everyone is around. It's all designed to get everyone's attention. Surely everyone walking by will applaud and say, "Now there is a righteous man. He is praying openly, unashamedly, and his use of words is so fantastic." Jesus' comment on that picture might be, "I sure hope you enjoyed the applause, Mr. Pharisee, because that's all the reward you'll get. Anything done for the sole purpose of the applause of men will not be recognized in heaven."

A perverted consciousness of others is a dead giveaway to the existence of self-righteousness. God has designed us to be conscious of others, but to be conscious of others for their sake. One of the great blessings of being delivered from morbid self-consciousness is that we can live our lives for the sake of others (like the Good Samaritan). A perverted consciousness of others, however, means that we are aware of them for our own sake. In other words, we get some sense of satisfaction and identification from their applause and appreciation.

Someone has said that those whose motive is to get other people's applause are living secondhand lives. They are unable to do anything for the sheer pleasure of doing it. Everything is done for what is said of them. This is not high-level living.

JUSTICE FOR OTHERS, MERCY FOR ME

In one of my favorite stories of the whole Bible, we have Jesus again exposing an aspect of self-righteousness. We commonly call this the story of the prodigal son.[14] Actually, it was told by Jesus, and the star of the story is the second son. It goes something like this:

A father had two sons. The younger wanted to get his inheritance early, asked for it, and got it. He went away and wasted his inheritance on scandalous living. He finally came to the end of himself, and while feeding swine in a hog pen, this young Jewish lad decided to go home to his father. When he got home, his father ran to meet him in the road, put his own garments on him, put shoes on his feet, put a ring on his finger, killed the fatted calf, and declared a feast in his honor.

That's a great story and many truths can be learned about the nature of a loving father and his rebellious kids, but the climax of the story is yet to come.

It's the older son who is the point of the story. When he sees the father responding in mercy toward this obvious sinner, he is offended. The younger son has made some terrible decisions. First of all, he dishonored his father by asking for his inheritance before his father's death. Second, he misused all his resources and, therefore, proved to be a very unfaithful steward. Third, he dishonored the family by being a part of an industry that was rejected in their society—feeding swine. Fourth, he had the audacity to come home and show his face after doing such dastardly deeds.

On the other hand, the older son saw himself as the model child. He had stayed home, worked hard, and sought to please his father. But he had defined life incorrectly. He thought he could please his father by working hard and keeping all the rules when, all along, what the father wanted was to share everything he owned with his son. The older son, in his blindness, exposes one of the hidden attributes of self-righteousness— a demand of justice for others.

I don't know about others, but I find this aspect of self-righteousness still hanging around in me. I surely want God to treat me with mercy, but I have a tendency to want others to get what they deserve. This tendency can express itself in something as small as being offended when someone cuts me off in a lane on the freeway or in harboring resentment toward those who've been promoted when I've been overlooked. Sometimes it becomes the impetus for a pity party, where I mournfully tell God that I've tried to do right and that I've gotten very little benefit, while those who have seemingly disregarded His way and Word are recognized and blessed with the rewards of earth and heaven.

UNTEACHABLE DEFENSIVENESS

Is there no end to this? How big is this thing of self-righteousness? Well, in actuality, it's bigger than we'll have room in this chapter to examine. There is one final aspect of self-righteousness we'll examine, and it is one that is obvious. The self-righteous person is unteachable. This was exposed in the Pharisees when Jesus told a parable that the Pharisees recognized was aimed directly at them.[15] Jesus told the parable to show that those who had rejected the mercy of God were themselves going to be rejected by God. The Pharisees' response was typical of a self-righteous attitude:

> When the chief priests and the Pharisees heard Jesus' parables, they knew he was talking about them. They looked for a way to arrest him, but they were afraid of the crowd because the people held that he was a prophet.[16]

This response of the Pharisees stands in contrast to that of our friend Ralph in John, chapter 9. Ralph was not much of a theologian. He actually didn't know much about this Jesus who had healed him, but when Jesus found him after all the inquisition, He asked Ralph if he believed in the Messiah. Ralph's teachable response was:

"Who is he, sir? Tell me so that I may believe in him."[17]

The truly righteous are always looking for truth in order to trade up. The self-righteous believe they already have it and are not interested in the trade.

These are not all the aspects of self-righteousness, I'm sure. It seems that every day of my life I can find some new nuances of this hideous obstacle. Maybe these will give an idea of how pervasive self-righteousness was in the days that Eternal Life walked on the earth in the form of Jesus, the Son of God, and give us some clues to detect it and expose it to the light of His life. Then we can trade self-righteousness for the righteousness that comes by faith.

Some may ask, "Why does God leave this counterfeit around?" Remember, every obstacle exists to reduce us to a faith that discovers Jesus to be more than we thought. Jesus is real life. He totally satisfies. When we have settled for the counterfeit, dry dullness will remind us there is more.

Guilt and the Condemning Heart

There are two more major obstacles that stop many from enjoying the consciousness of God's presence. They both have to do with sin. One is guilt. The other is the condemning heart. There are many Scriptures that lead us to believe that sin still keeps us out of the presence of God.

Surely the arm of the LORD is not too short to save, nor his ear too dull to hear. But your iniquities have separated you from your God; your sins have hidden his face from you, so that he will not hear.[18]

A casual interpretation of this passage leaves us somewhat hesitant to rush boldly into the presence of God.

What exactly is guilt? Well, there are whole volumes in psychology written on the subject, but for our purposes we will define it as the internal conflict resulting from violating the eternal laws of God's order which are written in the human heart, in created nature, and in the Old and New Testaments. Guilt is the result of violating absolute standards of God's order. Some have tried to rid themselves of guilt by denying the existence of the standards. It just doesn't work. They are built into our makeup. The only way to get rid of true guilt is by death. So, we have two choices: our death or His. Guilt can't be treated successfully by denial, penance, or good works. God's judgment is clear:

The wages of sin is death.[19]

The good news is that Jesus has died and we can be free from the guilt of our sins by placing our trust in the already shed blood of Jesus. It is our faith in the blood of Jesus that gives us entrance into His eternal presence. Nothing else is a fitting sacrifice. If God requires death, then it is reprehensible that we should offer something as common as our works.

Because by one sacrifice he has made perfect forever those who are being made holy.[20]

Therefore, brothers, since we have confidence to enter the Most Holy Place by the blood of Jesus…[21]

The condemning heart, on the other hand, is the counterfeit of guilt. God built in guilt to let us know something is wrong so that we can come to Him to fix it. But the condemning heart produces feelings of failure and shame resulting from violating the conscience that is not aligned with the reality of God's mercy.

Therefore, there is now no condemnation for those who are in Christ Jesus.[22]

Since we put our trust in the shed blood of Jesus, the just laws of God cannot condemn us. Any condemnation must then come from the counterfeiter, or from our hearts that are not cleansed from the effects of the fall of man.

Little children, let us not love with word or with tongue, but in deed and truth. We will know by this that we are of the truth, and will assure our heart before Him in whatever our heart condemns us; for God is greater than our heart and knows all things.

Beloved, if our heart does not condemn us, we have confidence before God; and whatever we ask we receive from Him, because we keep His commandments and do the things that are pleasing in His sight.[23]

The options given in these verses are obvious. We can be condemned or confident. The issue is what can be done with a condemning heart.

"Let your conscience be your guide" is a good place to start in teaching our young to recognize the value of integrity, but it is not the highest level of guidance we have as believers in Christ. Our conscience can be and is colored by values and norms of our culture. It too must be brought to alignment with the word of God. The good news of this passage is that God is greater than our hearts and we can appeal to Him. He specializes in real mercy, not fairness or cheap grace. (For a further study of this subject, see my book *Grace Works*.)

When these obstacles crop up, we should make a mad dash for the mercy revealed in the death and resurrection of Jesus. Our confidence is based on God's justice being satisfied by the death of Jesus. We actually have legal rights to enter into His presence. The fact that Jesus is now alive means we can actually visit with Him. He can overrule our hearts and cleanse us so that our hearts align with His word. We can, in effect, appeal to a higher authority to get a more accurate judgment. Culture has trained our internal governor (conscience), but God's judgment is constant.

First, we appeal to His word as revealed in Scripture. To violate the clear teaching of Scripture is to incur real guilt. To submit to the authority of Scripture is to invite the Holy Spirit to convict of sin and cast out the unholy spirit of condemnation.

If Scripture does not give a specific answer, we then submit to the limitations of love. Realizing that, in Christ, we have been liberated from the external restrictions of law, we submit to living for the blessings of others rather than just for ourselves.

"Everything is permissible"—but not everything is beneficial. "Everything is permissible"—but not everything is constructive.[24]

Love expressed is a sure antidote for condemnation.

Dear children, let us not love with words or tongue but with actions and in truth. This then is how we know that we belong to the truth, and how we set our hearts at rest in his presence whenever our hearts condemn us. For God is greater than our hearts, and he knows everything.[25]

It is futile to argue with a condemning heart. Appeal to the final judge. Accept His decision and go love someone!

These obstacles are constantly rearing their heads. Our response when confronted with self-righteousness is to seek more of God's righteousness. When guilt is present, we seek forgiveness. And when our heart condemns us, we run to Jesus to find freedom. This way the obstacles become our friends. They give us opportunities to find more in Jesus than we knew before!

CHAPTER FOUR

THE ATTITUDE
THAT GETS
GOD'S ATTENTION

For this is what the high and lofty One sayhr—he who lives forever,
whose name is holy: "I live in a high and holy place, but also with him who is
contrite and lowly in spirit, to revive the spirit of the lowly and
to revive the heart of the contrite."

ISAIAH 57:15

For centuries, the key to travel and work in the world was the horse. But as beautiful an animal as the horse is, it is useless until broken. There's aesthetic value in watching the wild mustang range over the open prairie, but not until its strength, intelligence, and loyalty are harnessed by a master does the horse fulfill its greatest destiny.

Human beings have a lot of potential, too. We have been created to bear the image of God. We have been equipped with the intelligence, creativity, and strength to rule the created world. Since the fall of original man, however, we too are wild and untamed. Until broken we will, at best, be unfulfilled potential—and at worst become the destroyers of the world.

Brokenness is not a very popular word. It sounds harsh, painful, and even destructive. We tend to omit it from our vocabulary and shun it as an experience. But if we could talk to the horses, we might find that it is not as bad to be under the care of a loving master as we might think. Maybe we can't talk to horses, but we can hear from those who have lived their lives under the control of the Master. Paul called himself a bondservant, a good term for brokenness.[1] So did James[2] and Peter.[3] Those throughout history who have yielded totally to God's yoke have found life at its best.

"Come to me, all you who are weary and burdened, and I will give you rest. Take my yoke upon you and learn from me, for I am gentle and humble in heart, and you will find rest for your souls. For my yoke is easy and my burden is light."[4]

The natural question that arises is, "Why do we need to be broken?" Aren't we basically good and, if freed from all our prejudices and fears, would we not fulfill our destiny on the earth? The answer to that is, *"No."* Because of the Fall, we too must be broken. Recently, several hundred thousand people in America watched a movie called *The Horse Whisperer.* It's a story of a horse that went through the trauma of an accident, then was healed by the skill of a loving master. The story line of the movie reveals this master as having some innate sense of being able to communicate to the horse his love and acceptance, thereby bringing the horse through its fears to achieve its original purpose.

God created us with great capacities to represent Him on the earth, but we too were wounded, scarred, and scared. If we go back and read the account of Adam and Eve in the garden, we find them hiding behind a bush after they have sinned. When God asked Adam why, he revealed the deep wound of sin.

"I was afraid because I was naked; so I hid."[5]

God made us with needs designed to draw us into intimacy with Him. He gave us a need for security so that we would come to Him in total dependence and find our security in relationship. He gave us a need to belong so that we would long to be a part of God's people and be will-ing to relate to other brothers and sisters in creation. He gave us a need for significance so that we would find our sense of self-worth in Him. It is as if God were the positive pole of the magnet, creating us as the nega-tive pole so that we would be drawn to Him. However, in the Fall, we were so wounded, ashamed, and scared that, instead of running toward God to have our needs met, we ran away. In running away, we replaced the faith that God desires with our humanistic substitute, presumption.

PRESUMPTION
GREED, GANGS, AND GOALS

Made to depend upon God, we continue to insist on our independence and try to meet our needs outside of His order. Instead of finding our security in our loving dependence upon God, we have found it in our greed. We have bought the lie that the abundance of the things we possess will give us security. We continue to gather money, land, houses, and cars, even though Jesus said possessions are so temporal they could be removed by a moth or rust or a thief. Instead of having our need to belong met by relating properly to others of the human race, we have resorted to our own personal gangs.

Not all gangs are on the street. There are some down at the country club. There are some over at the church. They are in every aspect of life. We tend to segregate ourselves from others because they are different from us. We find our own sense of belonging with those who look like us, talk like us, and act like us, and we wind up a member of the gang.

Instead of doing the will of God and finding our significance in partnership with Him, we have replaced that great privilege by becoming men and women of goals. We set goals for everything and then try to find some sense of significance by meeting them, measuring them with others, and giving ourselves trophies for our achievements. *Greed, gangs,* and *goals* will never satisfy the deep longing that God has put within our hearts…but we keep trying. Scripture gives clear evidence that presumption in any form is destructive and alienates us from God.

God, through Moses, warned of the dire consequences to those who would try to speak for God without God's warrant.[6] Since God created us to represent Him on earth, there's something innate within us that makes us want to speak for God. But to speak for God when God hasn't spoken is a clear act of presumption. It may gain us some recognition among our peers, but it gains us nothing but rebuke from God Himself.

I should note that it is not the sin of presumption for us to commit ourselves to the body of Christ and ask for input as we learn to practice the spiritual gifts that God has released to the body. Sometimes the fear of presumption has caused some to not even want to practice a gift like prophesy or discernment when, in fact, the apostle Paul has encouraged us all to practice and perfect our gifts to encourage one another. Yet the Scriptures give ample warning to those who want to build their reputations as prophets and seers and who may be tempted to speak more directly than they've heard.

OUR AGENDA, OUR CALENDAR

We see another expression of presumption after the children of Israel were instructed by God to go in and take the Promised Land He had given them. They were afraid and refused to go. However, on the next day they decided that they would do what the Lord had told them to do the day before. This was not a good idea.[7] Anytime we try to do God's will on our agenda and our calendar, we are guilty of presumption. When the seed is sowed on the hard soil and it is not immediately received, it is plucked away by Satan. In our society, where everything seems to bend to our own agendas of comfort and convenience, we will find that many times God's commands to us are neither convenient nor comfortable. If we insist on obeying God in our own way we are guilty of the sin of presumption.

EGALITARIAN DEMANDS

There's another expression of presumption from the time that Moses was leading the children of Israel. Moses was the God-appointed leader of Israel. Korah and his friends assumed authority not given to them by God.

> They came as a group to oppose Moses and Aaron and said to them, "You have gone too far! The whole community is holy, every one of them, and the LORD is with them. Why then do you set yourselves above the LORD'S assembly?"[8]

Korah, like many people today, had been infected by the myth of egalitarianism, expressing itself in the refusal to acknowledge a distinction between leaders and followers. This attitude demands that everything must be equal and equally shared. Out of this kind of ideology comes disrespect for leaders and the belief that everyone has the same amount of authority. Moses responded to Korah and his friends by telling them that God would show whom He had chosen to be leader. He essentially said that if anyone died a natural death on the next day they would all know that Moses was not the leader—but if God took some people supernaturally they would know that God had anointed Moses leader.

As you read that story, you'll see that the earth opened up and swallowed those who were resisting Moses.[9] It is an eternal testimony that

God is not really high on the presumptuous attitude of assuming authority not given by God.

'RESPECTABLE' TITLES

As we move to the New Testament, we see some other examples of presumption and God's attitude toward it. Jesus was straightforward as He spoke to the Pharisees about their desiring respectable titles.[10] They wanted to be called leader, father, and teacher. These titles carried with them great respect among the people. It was the respect that the Pharisees were addicted to, not the responsibility of serving that those titles depicted. A person who wants the title of "leader" wants to be able to say, "Everyone fall in behind me. I'm running the show." Jesus makes it very clear that in His kingdom the leaders will be the servants of all.

"Father" is always a respectable title, and the Pharisees also wanted to be respected because of their age. Their attitude was, "Because I am older, I know more than you." As badly as we need real fathers today to bring spiritual children along to maturity, we do not need any more people who simply want the title of father, but are unwilling to serve behind the scenes raising up the children and doing whatever it takes to bring them to maturity.

The Pharisees also wanted to be called "teachers," because in being a teacher their attitude was, "Because I know more than you I deserve to lead; therefore, I am superior." We can thank God for all the teachers in the body of Christ, but there again we don't need those who want the title of teacher yet are unwilling to serve by diligently studying the Scripture, spending time with God, and delivering to us the instructions that come straight from Him. For all of those who want titles in order to make them feel significant, Jesus gives His solution:

"The greatest among you will be your servant."[11]

SECURITY IN STUFF

Another New Testament illustration of a form of presumption is found in the story that Jesus told about the rich, young fool.[12] This is a story about a man who had just brought in his crops and found that he had more goods than he had barns to contain them. So he counseled with himself and decided that he would build more barns and store up more stuff in order to increase his security level. His attitude was, "So, you have many goods laid up for many years to come. Take your ease. Eat, drink, and be merry." God's response to him was, "You fool. This very night your soul is required of you, and now who will own what you have prepared?"

Our whole society is filled with people who have fallen for the deceitfulness of riches, the concept that we can trust the things we own to get us through tough times. In times of plenty, it is easy to be deceived by this lie. We can convince ourselves that we really trust God when, in fact, we have plenty of goods around. It is when the possession of those goods is threatened that we find out if we have allowed our heart to be attached to them. I think many times God allows a shortage in order for us to know that we've been deceived by riches.

BUSINESS VS. PERSONAL LIFE

Still another illustration of presumption is found in the teachings of James, which speak of businessmen who built their future on going to a certain city and doing business.[13] His instruction is that we should say: "If God wills we will do these things." The implication is that these people are making business plans without consulting God's agenda.

Those who have separated their business world from their religious world are presumptuous. There is no warrant for the dualistic idea that our personal and family life is to be governed by the kingdom of God, while our business life is to be governed by the world's rules of business. In the kingdom of God, every aspect of our life is to be brought under the order of that kingdom. Jesus is king over everything, including our business life. If He is not consulted about what we do there, then we obviously are not submitted to Him. When businesses, as well as businesspeople, reflect the character of God's kingdom, real Christianity is on display.

OUR OWN RIGHTEOUSNESS

The last illustration we will look at is the story that Jesus told about the presumptuous man who looked with contempt upon those who did not live as he lived.[14] Jesus told about a Pharisee who went to the temple, prayed to himself because of all the good things that he did, and looked with contempt upon a poor tax collector who did not live by the expected laws. How easy it is for us to judge those who do not live by our rules of righteousness and to consider ourselves in a better position with God than they.

Actually, the one who is in the best position with God is the one who recognizes his deep need for God and for continually coming to Him in total dependence. After all, that is why all of our needs were given to us—to draw us to a dependent relationship with God so that we could know Him and enjoy Him forever. The poor tax collector who recognized his need and relied on God for mercy is the one who went back to his home justified that day, rather than the man who presumed that he was right with God because he had lived up to his own definition of righteousness.

Brokenness

God's love will not permit us to continue to live in presumption. He is determined to bring us to a position of dependence upon Him. Herein lies our highest freedom. This is brokenness.

"But what does brokenness look like?" someone may ask. "Are we supposed to spend all of our lives as the tax collector did, unwilling to lift his face in the presence of God and always berating ourselves because we are no good?" Well, let's see if we can find a biblical description of brokenness. The Old Testament picture of brokenness is like this:

This is what the LORD says: "Heaven is my throne, and the earth is my footstool. Where is the house you will build for me?

Where will my resting place be? Has not my hand made all these things, and so they came into being?" declares the LORD.

"This is the one I esteem: he who is humble and contrite in spirit, and trembles at my word."[15]

The New Testament description of brokenness sounds like this:

If anyone considers himself religious and yet does not keep a tight rein on his tongue, he deceives himself and his religion is worthless. Religion that God our Father accepts as pure and faultless is this: to look after orphans and widows in their distress and to keep oneself from being polluted by the world.[16]

A HUMBLE HEART

Out of these two passages we can find four characteristics of biblical brokenness. First, a humble heart—a heart that is conscious of the presence of someone greater. One does not have to try to be humble when one is consciously in the presence of someone greater. When we are aware that we live our lives in the presence of the God of this universe, we do not tend to put on a show or act in presumption. It is when we lose consciousness of His presence that we begin to exalt ourselves and to live as if He were not there. Those who are trying to appear humble when they are not conscious of the presence of a big God are simply guilty of false humility, another form of presumption.

A CONTRITE SPIRIT

The second characteristic of brokenness is called a contrite spirit. I believe it's the same quality that Jesus was talking about when He began His Sermon on the Mount with the Beatitudes:

"Blessed are the poor in spirit, for theirs is the kingdom of heaven."[17]

To be poor in spirit is to recognize that our only advantage with God is that we're needy and that He is full of mercy. Donald McCullough said, "The poor in spirit know they have lost control, should never have tried to take control, and never again want control."[18] The word *poor* used here by Jesus depicts one who has nothing, knows that he has nothing, is willing to admit that he has nothing, and realizes that if he ever has anything it will be because of mercy. The poor in spirit must accept God on His own terms because, in fact, they are not able to make Him live on their terms.

A BRIDLED TONGUE

The third characteristic of brokenness is a bridled tongue. Until we come to realize that the greatest weapon on earth is not a nuclear bomb or laser power, but actually is a member of the human body, the tongue, we are as dangerous as a monkey with a loaded gun.

A friend of mine, Duane Blue, recently told the story of his life at a conference. He related that he was abandoned by his father in early childhood. His mother tried to rear him, but he grew up rebellious and angry at the world. In order to survive, he learned to use his tongue as a mighty weapon. He was able to successfully defend himself in any situation because of the skill of his nasty tongue.

Duane used his tongue many times on his lonely and confused mom. One day he found his mother dead on the bathroom floor. She had taken her own life, but Duane knew in his heart that he had contributed to her death with the skillful use of his most powerful weapon.

Duane continued telling the conference audience his story of loneliness and confusion and of the gracious redemption that he'd since found in Jesus Christ. As he concluded his story, he offered his listeners the same mercy that had saved him from a life of isolation and confusion. Then he said, "Some of you tonight will reject the offer of grace, and I ask you to do me a favor. When you get to hell, please tell my mother, 'I'm sorry.'"

My own heart was pierced by that story from Duane. I realized that I had been guilty of claiming that I yielded to the Master's control when my tongue was revealing something totally different. God wants to bring a brokenness into our lives that makes us candidates to get our prayers answered. That kind of brokenness controls the tongue.

AN 'OTHERS' FOCUS

The fourth characteristic of biblical brokenness is an "others" focus—a willingness to live for the benefit of someone outside ourselves. James couches it in the language of visiting orphans and widows, but I think he would include anyone in obvious need. Real brokenness takes the focus off us and puts it somewhere else.

How Are We Broken?

The next major question that crops up is, "How does it happen?" Shall we return to the corral and listen again to the horses? Two of them were discussing their brokenness one day. "When were you broken?" the sorrel asked the paint.

"Well," said the paint, "I shall never forget that day. I was running wild in the pasture when this cowboy rode up on another horse, threw a rope around my neck, and tied me to his saddlehorn. Boy, did I buck! I bucked for hours. Finally, he put me into a corral and tied me to a post. I tried my best to get away from that rope, but I could not break it.

"On the next day, he came out with several other cowboys and tied me down while they placed a blanket and a saddle on my back. Man, that felt terrible. I began to buck and strain against the pressure that was put upon me. Then they hoisted another cowboy into the saddle and turned me loose. I tried with all of my energy to unseat him and to get that horrible saddle off my back. I bucked and ran and jumped. I threw the cowboy off several times, but he kept getting back on.

"Finally, I realized I was unable to buck him off, and I began to yield to his pressure. I slowly began to trot around the corral as he pulled me around with bit and bridle. It took several more weeks for me to get accustomed to someone being on my back and someone else being in charge of my life. I would have to say that those were the worst weeks of my life. But the fact is, I am now broken and I wouldn't trade anything for it. I love my master and I love working as a partner with him."

Then the paint turned to the sorrel. "What about you? Tell me about your brokenness experience."

The sorrel said, "My story wasn't much like yours. I too was running wild in the pasture. The cowboy would come up every day and whistle at me. For several days I ignored his whistle. Then one day I sensed that he had something to give me. I got close enough to smell that he had some red apples in his hand. He tossed them over and I munched on them. The next time he came out, I came all the way up to him and ate sugar out of his hand. We did that for several days until one day he gently placed a halter over my neck. It felt a little strange, but I had already grown accustomed to his hand.

"A few days later the cowboy led me into the corral. I had never been confined quite like that and I was a little uncomfortable, but because I was beginning to trust the cowboy I was able to stay without great fear. One day, while feeding me sugar from his hand, he placed a blanket over my back and led me around. I had never had a blanket over my back, but it wasn't so bad.

"A few days after that, on top of the blanket, the cowboy added a saddle. This was a little heavier—but after all, by now I was beginning to trust the cowboy. If he wanted me to carry a saddle, so be it.

"Then one day, after patting me on the neck and giving me another apple, the cowboy climbed into the saddle. I was a little spooked because I had never had anyone that heavy on my back before. But I didn't buck and yank. I awkwardly walked around with the one I had come to know riding on my back. There were several weeks of training and I learned how and what he wanted me to do. This process took place over a matter of several weeks. Actually, I don't know which one of those days you could say I was broken, but today I know I'm broken and I wouldn't trade anything for it."

This apocryphal story is intended to give us some clue that God doesn't use the same method to break us all. The point is that He wants us to be totally submissive to His hand. God's desire for us can be summed up as the following:

> *I will instruct you and teach you in the way you should go;*
> *I will counsel you and watch over you.*
> *Do not be like the horse or the mule,*
> *which have no understanding*
> *but must be controlled by bit and bridle*
> *or they will not come to you.*[19]

PERSONAL FAILURE

One of the ways God breaks us is through personal failure. We find this happening many times in Scripture. David is a great example in the Old Testament. Through his personal failure and brokenness he found the mercy of God. In the New Testament it was Peter who, out of his presumptuous attitude, professed that he would never deny the Lord, yet found himself totally exposed before the next morning was over. He, too, was broken—and in his brokenness, found usefulness as he took the gospel to the Gentiles and became one of the pillars of the early church.

Watchman Nee said:

God allows that soul to fall, to weaken, and even to sin that he may understand whether or not any good resides in the flesh. This usually happens to one who thinks he's progressing spiritually. The Lord tries him in order that he may know himself. It is altogether a most difficult lesson and is not learned within a day or a night. Only after many years does one come to realize how untrustworthy is his flesh.[20]

Our personal failures were never designed by God to bring us to a place of being crushed, wounded, and useless. They were designed to bring us to a place where we no longer trust ourselves, but God only. It is then that we are useful and the potential that God has placed in us can be tapped for His purposes.

BURDENS TOO GREAT

Sometimes God simply allows burdens beyond our personal strength to be placed upon us. Evidently this was the case with the apostle Paul, who had the "thorn in his flesh." This thorn was such a nuisance to Paul that he was determined that God needed to remove it. Instead, God gave him extra grace to face it.

Sometimes brokenness comes through the unexplainable sufferings of life. The hardship of living in a fallen world can bring about circumstances that bring us to the end of ourselves.

THE REVELATION OF MERCY

No matter what circumstances create the soil for brokenness, the only thing that brings ultimate brokenness in our lives is a revelation of the unconditional love and mercy of Jesus. The author of Hebrews mentions that Jesus died outside the gates.[21] When our vision of Him outside the gates is etched in our hearts, then we are broken. For we see then that in reality, He was broken for us.

To die outside the gates of the city meant that one was an alien (that is, not a part of the covenant community), a criminal, or a leper. When Jesus was crucified outside the gates for us He took all of our crimes; Jesus took upon Himself every law of the kingdom that we have broken so that we would no longer have to bear the burden of being a criminal.

He also took our moral leprosy, the perversion that is in our life because of the sickness of our own selfish sin. We no longer have to live with the sense of being dirty, perverted, and demented. Jesus took that place for us so that we would not have to. He also took the place of the alien, the one separated from the covenant people because they were not children of promise.

We are included into the people of God because He took our place outside the people of God. When the Holy Spirit pulls the veil from our eyes to let us see Jesus in our place as a criminal, moral leper, and alien, we find the real heart of brokenness. When the crushing blows of life have battered our hearts, we can always run to Him who reminds us that He was broken for us. We can be broken by mercy and not crushed by judgment. It is our choice: we can fall on the Rock and be broken, or we can resist, the Rock will fall on us, and we will be crushed.

RUN TO JESUS

Well, what are we to do to be broken? The answer is simple, but not simplistic. It is simply to run to Jesus. All of life, the good and the bad, is designed to get us into intimacy with God so that we can enjoy Him and then, through that joy, express His glory in all the world. It is in the arms of Jesus that we find the unconditional love that brings us the security that we were designed to have.

In those same arms of Jesus we find our ability to be sociable and to relate to other brothers and sisters. It is in the arms of Jesus that we find true significance—we are sons of the kingdom, ambassadors from heaven, and children of God. With the attitude produced by this recognition we can live and pray. And when we pray, our prayers—our incense—are answered with thunder.

The sacrifices of God are a broken spirit;
a broken and contrite heart,
O God, you will not despise.[22]

Father, we are aware that we resist brokenness. Thank you for introducing us to it anyway. Make our soul responsive to your Spirit so that your "eye" guides us rather than the bit and bridle.

CHAPTER FIVE

CONFIDENT PRAYING

W e pray as we live. To try to pray confidently while living in fear is futility. On the other hand, any act of living—when done in the name of Jesus—is a form of prayer.

Michelle was convinced that she was a poor prayer warrior. She'd been asked to join her church's prayer team. *I just don't make prayer enough of a priority,* she lamented. *I use all my energy trying to keep three kids in school and my husband happy. I intend every day to pray more, but I fall into bed every night feeling exhausted and guilty.*

I am sure there are hundreds like Michelle. To all who battle such thoughts: *There is hope.* Each responsibility can be turned into a prayer when done in Jesus' name. Every act of obedience becomes a prayer. Our challenge is to live like we pray and pray like we live, so that our lives are prayers as much as the speeches we direct toward heaven.

The model prayer Jesus gave the disciples is also a model life. We can't pray "hallowed be thy name" if we don't *live* "hallowed be thy name." Prayer is spectacular in its effect but ordinary in its form. We will err if we elevate prayer to some form of spirituality that can only be achieved by some idealized super-saint. The real work is done by the ordinary people who have discovered the extraordinary privilege of linking heaven and earth through prayer.

Rosemary Rutland has captured the hidden reality of the apparent "ordinariness" of prayer.

I'm terrified of growing up. I guess you could say that I'm the poster child for the "Peter Pan concept." I look at the women of my mother's generation and quake in fear. If I allow myself to grow up, then before I know it, I'll be joining the Junior League. Covered dish isn't my idea of a fun time and I have every intention of making sure that my social life doesn't revolve around Sunday School parties, or at least, that was how I used to feel. Then, God orchestrated an evening that would shake me to the core and change my perception of what it means to be a woman and a mother.

You see, every summer I go to Youth Advance as a counselor. The one part about being a camp counselor that I don't like is praying with my girls at the altar. They need so much help and I'm not exactly a spiritual giant. I try to make sure that I end up praying for one that feels bad about being mean to her kid brother. That is about all I can handle.

One night at the altar, I ended up, quite by accident, praying for the problem child of the camp. She wore a dog collar and a spiked bracelet. Her clothes were all black, and fishnet hose were her favorite accessory. She always wore knee high combat boots and demonic jewelry. I was the last person on earth that could help this child; she needed a prayer warrior, not a drama major.

I began to pray for her and some other kids came over and laid hands on her. She started shaking and I realized that God was breaking in on this girl's war-torn spirit. In other words, my worst nightmare. I was frantically searching for someone to help me out so I sent one of the other campers running for a pastor. Those guys are always dying for a piece of the spiritual action, and I was willing to share the wealth.

A pastor came and helped me carry the little girl into a nearby room and then left me. I turned around to discover that the "capable hands" he had left me in were two of my mother's best friends. Good grief! God was punishing me for everything wrong that I had ever done. I had a child that was obviously personally acquainted with Legion himself, I was about to have bladder failure, and my only help was two women who think homemade lasagna and a big hug could solve Ted Bundy's problems.

I was about to hyperventilate, and was looking around for a paper bag, when something amazing happened. These two ordinary women that I have known since I took my first breath suddenly became veritable shape shifters. With a quiet intensity that

I had never known, they began to pray for the girl. They were calling out spirits and commanding Satan to leave this child's body. I wasn't too quick and it took me a second to realize that I was in the room with greatness. I was sitting in the room with two women that are prayer warriors of a stature I could only hope to attain. Those ladies did not for one second experience the fear that was eating me alive.

You see, they had been facing Satan for years. Every time they leaned over the bed of one of their children and prayed God's purpose for his or her life, they had faced Satan head on. Every time they sat up waiting for a teenager who was hours late for curfew and had bound Satan's control in that rebellious life, they were involved in hand-to-hand combat. Each prayer for God to work His purpose in their children's lives was a threat to the hierarchy of hell. Every prayer for God to guide a Christian spouse to their children was a direct challenge to Lucifer.

I thought of all the times I had seen them start their day with a simple devotion and coffee. These women looked like ordinary housewives, and yet, they waged war each day for their children.

I sat there watching those ladies bind the demonic powers in that young life with power. One of them began to remove the child's spiked bracelet and satanic jewelry. The other lady struggled to remove the little girl's heavy combat boots. I will never forget the look on her face as she jerked on the laces of those boots. It was then that I understood that these women were committed to fighting for us. They were using the only weapons they had…good homes, strong marriages, big hugs, hot lasagna, and hours spent in prayer…for their own children, for their friends' children, and for nameless kids like this little girl wearing a dog collar. They were fighting for us, an entire generation of kids who are scared to death of our own lives and of our own futures.

All of a sudden, I would have given anything in the world to be just like them. They possessed a bravery I wanted to have. Everybody comes to a point when they just know it's time to grow up. That night, watching two of my "other mothers" help that little girl, I realized that I had to go about the task of growing up, because they weren't going to be around forever and one day there was going to be another generation of kids that would need women who are willing to give their lives over to the task of fighting for them. In twenty years there will be my kids, my friends' kids, and some little girl wearing a dog collar that will need women that have poured themselves into battling for the lives of children, and I'm going to have to be one of them. I just hope that God can build something in me that's capable of doing the job and that I can find a decent recipe for lasagna.[1]

We are encouraged by several Scriptures to be confident in our approach toward God.

Dear friends, if our hearts do not condemn us, we have confidence before God and receive from him anything we ask, because we obey his commands and do what pleases him.[2]

This is the confidence we have in approaching God: that if we ask anything according to his will, he hears us. And if we know that he hears us—whatever we ask—we know that we have what we asked of him.[3]

Three Pillars of Confident Praying

It seems that our Father wants us to be certain that praying is not a laborious or fearful thing, but rather is the expression of one's life—one who is confident in his relationship with God. There are three pillars to the foundation of confident praying.

First of all, we must be convinced that God is willing to share His dominion with us. God has decreed that we are His vice regents on earth. He is going to make His will known on earth through us. This imparted dignity should give us confidence when we go before Him. We don't go as beggars who need something for survival; rather, we go as those who are in the family business with our heavenly Father. This is not a false confidence that springs from shoring ourselves up by self-talk, but a confidence that comes from a foundational truth: God created us in His own image and gave us the mandate to subdue this earth under God's control.[4]

The second pillar of confident praying is that God has done a work of reconciliation that makes it possible for us to live in constant communication with Him. His mandate to subdue the earth would be impossible if we did not have access to God's wisdom. The fact that, through Jesus Christ, God has made it possible for us to share in His very life is again a great reason for confidence. We can never forget that our entrance into the presence of God is by the shed blood of Jesus, not by anything we have or that we have done. We must overcome our tendency to doubt the good news that God has once and for all accepted the shed blood of Jesus as a sacrifice for all of our sins.

The third pillar of truth for confident praying is that we can know that we pray the will of God. "According to Thy will" has been an obstacle to many because they weren't convinced that they could know the will of God. Many prayers have been offered with feeble confidence because of this unbelief. Maybe it would help us if we reaffirmed our belief that everything starts with God.

> For from him and through him and to him are all things. To him
> be glory forever! Amen.[5]

Ambassadors of God

Prayer is not something that people thought up. It is an idea that came out of the very thoughts of God. Obviously, God is sovereign enough that He can do anything without allowing us to participate—yet He has chosen to let us have that privilege in His work on earth. He did not give us a burden we couldn't handle. It is not our job to decide everything that needs to be done. It is our job to hear what He wants done and carry it out. In this way we act as real ambassadors of God.

One of the great illustrations of this was in the story of Jesus' first miracle.[6] He and His mother had gone to a wedding feast. The hostess had run out of wine during the feast and had asked Mary, Jesus' mother, for help. Mary went to Jesus and made a very discerning and accurate request. She simply said, "They're out of wine." It's interesting that Mary didn't tell Jesus how to fix the problem. She simply brought the problem to Him and left to His discretion and resources the way to fix it.

We could learn a lot from Mary's approach to prayer. In its essence, prayer is the work of the Holy Spirit in us, bringing us into partnership with the work of the Trinity on earth. We can be sure that the Holy Spirit always works according to the sovereign purposes of God. When our ear is attuned to His guidance, we will know when it's time to pray, and we'll have some indication of what to pray. Then we will have the faith to leave the results in His hands. The Scriptures clearly teach that the pattern works like this: Whatever the Father initiates, the Son carries out, and then the Holy Spirit makes it real in our lives (compare Ephesians 1:11 and 2 Thessalonians 2:13).

The Life of Christ

The life that we were given is actually the life of Christ. Through the miracle of regeneration we have been changed. We live by the power of the indwelling Holy Spirit.

This is a difficult statement for many to understand, but the truth is we have not just received a life that we are told to model after Christ—

we actually have received His life.[7]

Jesus exhibited life guided by God's purposes. As He walked through the land of Palestine, He healed some, but not all. He raised some of the dead, but not each one. He delivered some from demonic influences, but not all. He did not directly address all of the ills of society.

Some have been offended that Jesus didn't address the practice of slavery as it existed in His day. Though He didn't address it directly, the foundation that He laid, by showing mercy to all people regardless of race, color, or creed, planted the seed that ultimately will destroy slavery. And though He didn't publicly address mistreatment of women, the dignity He showed His mother and the other women in His life planted the seeds that will ultimately destroy that discrimination.

Jesus refused to be controlled by the needs around Him. His only motivation was His Father's initiation. He truly gave us an example of a man guided by the Spirit. This is good news for us. If the only example we have in the New Testament is of Jesus, the Son of God, then there is not much hope for us mere humans. But the good news is that Jesus modeled for us the life of a man controlled by the Spirit of God. We can live like that.

Reality and the Holy Spirit

One of the wonderful privileges of being indwelt by the Holy Spirit is that we have access to the mind of God.

We have not received the spirit of the world but the Spirit who is from God, that we may understand what God has freely given us.[8]

Jesus said the Holy Spirit's ministry would lead us into all truth. Many times we limit the Holy Spirit's ministry to teaching us precepts from the Bible. I believe that His ministry is even larger than that, for it is the Holy Spirit's pleasure to lead us into reality. Reality is simply the way things are. When we think the way God thinks, we don't always have to depend only upon our reason and observation. The Holy Spirit gives us the privilege of looking through the apparent and seeing ultimate reality.

Jesus spoke to some unbelievers one day and told them that the reason they didn't believe was because "you are not my sheep."[9] Notice that Jesus didn't say, "You are not my sheep because you don't believe." He said as He looked at reality, "You don't believe because you are not one of my sheep." When God makes this kind of information available to us, it allows us to pray on a higher level than when we are simply operating on what our eyes can see and our ears can hear. It also prevents us from presumptuous praying. When we know the way things really are, we're not as apt to fall into the trap of trying to make something happen before its time.

It's interesting that when God spoke to Abraham, He said Abraham's descendants would spend four hundred years in slavery, but that they would, ultimately, come out in victory. God said they would come out at a time when the iniquity of the Amorites was full.[10] God had a timetable—and because Abraham was His servant and friend, He let him see through the apparent and into the real so that Abraham could both pray and live confidently and in peace. Abraham could endure the delay of blessings on his descendants and the injustice of a heathen nation because he knew the reality behind the apparent.

Sometimes those who give themselves zealously to prayer fall into the trap of praying only on the basis of what they see wrong and on their knowledge that God is a God of justice. They do not take into consideration that God has a timetable for a person's or a nation's wickedness to ripen.

I know people who are desperately praying for the conversion of the devil. Their thinking goes something like this: "God is a God of mercy and grace, the devil is in rebellion, God is not willing that any should perish, and so, if we are *really* compassionate and full of faith, we should pray for the conversion of the devil." I don't think we should spend a lot of our time praying for this. We've been given a glimpse by the Holy Spirit into the way things really are, and the devil is not going to be converted. We could waste a lot of energy praying for such things.

John encourages us to pray for our brother who is committing a sin not leading to death, but we are not encouraged to pray for our brother committing a sin leading to death.[11] Whatever may be our definition of a "sin leading to death," the issue is that we can know the reality of things—we can know when one has committed a sin unto death and when one hasn't. We're encouraged to pray with confidence for one, but not the other.

We must remember that prayer starts with God. We are not down here to try to get Him to do our will, but we are here to enforce His will. Therefore, our first responsibility and privilege is to discover what He wants done. In order to assist us in our confident praying, He is committed to revealing to us the way things are so that we can pray accordingly.

Pray as He Taught Us

We can know that we are praying according to the will of God when we pray as He taught us.

One day when the disciples asked Jesus to teach them to pray, He gave them a model that was much more than a set of words to say when we can't think of another prayer.[12] This model prayer from Jesus has been the subject of many books on prayer, yet the depth of its riches are still to be fathomed. When Jesus started the prayer with the phrase, "Hallowed be thy name," He was giving us a clue as to God's ultimate purpose.

It is God's ultimate purpose to glorify His name. To some that might seem like an egocentric motive for God. Yet it reveals His intimate knowledge of the life that He's given to us. The life that He's designed for us to live is a life best lived for the glory of another. It was patterned in the Trinity—the Father gave glory to the Son, the Son gave glory to the Father, and now the Holy Spirit gives glory to the Son who gives glory to the Father.

When we are brought into that fellowship, God gives us the privilege of spending our lives glorifying Him. He knows that's the only way we'll find the highest degree of our own fulfillment. So, in one sense, it is in our best self-interest to spend our lives glorifying God. It is an act of mercy that He gives us that privilege.

God's Mercy

Speaking of mercy, the aspect of God's character that He wants glorified the most is mercy.[13] God's essential nature is revealed most fully when He expresses mercy. The reputation He wants to promote is that He is on the side of the poor and needy. He is more than willing to meet us at the point of our legitimate need. It flies in the face of our natural pride when God says He doesn't want us to try to do anything for Him, but to trust Him to do for us what we cannot do for ourselves.[14]

When Bruce stood up recently in our local congregation and told of his miraculous cure from a disease that medical science had declared incurable, I think God's mercy got a better presentation than the forty-five-minute lecture I had given on the privilege of prayer. There might have been some skeptics present who would insist that it was a simple man's explanation to something that could be rationally figured out. But to all of those present who had needs of their own, it was a wonderful encouragement that God acts on behalf of the needy.

In the Old Testament it wasn't Israel's testimony of the great things they'd done for God that impressed their enemies; rather, it was what God had done for them. When the Israeli spies made it into Jericho they were questioned by Rahab, a prostitute of that city.[15] When she discovered that they represented Israel, she said to them, in effect, "Our nation trembles when we think of Israel, not because of who you are but because of your God. We have heard that your God feeds you with food from heaven, makes water run out of solid rock, and that when you go into battle He fights for you and all you have to do is show up. Our nation trembles at the thought of you because of the God who acts on your behalf" (my paraphrase). God's glory is most manifest when His mercy is received.

God tells His people Israel that He is not hungry for the meat that they're sacrificing and that all of their efforts at bringing Him bountiful sacrifices are not really what He wants. He gives them the essence of the matter when He says, "And call upon me in the day of trouble; I will deliver you, and you will honor me."[16] There's the surprise! The way we honor Him is by trusting in His mercy.

God's Provision for Our Needs

It's always been God's way to precede our need with His provision. In fact, it would be good for us to remember one of the eternal principles of God's ways: Our need is the prelude to His provision, which precedes our need. It's no secret to us that our needs get our attention turned toward God, but often we think that our need is the first thing on the scene. Actually, the presence of our need is God giving us an opportunity to discover His provision, which has been there all along.[17]

One of my dear friends and early mentors in ministry, Manley Beasley, asked me one time, "Dudley, which came first, your need or God's solution?" Since I knew he didn't ask foolish questions, I realized he was making a point. He went on to explain to me that God made water before He made fish, He made air before He made birds, and that Jesus was the lamb slain before the foundation of the earth.

When I get in trouble I don't have to send up a panic prayer to God, who then has to frantically get busy ordering heaven's workshop to solve my problem. Reality is that God knew of my need before the foundation of the earth, He already solved it in the person of His Son, Jesus Christ, and He's now willing to bring that solution into my life when I, by faith, can trust His mercy. If I could ever really assimilate that into my heart, it might change my daily attitude toward life. Instead of waking up with a sense of heavy burden, afraid of problems that might come during the day, I might actually look forward to them—knowing that God has already solved them and might allow one to show up so I can experience His glory.

If I truly understand the truth of His provision, I'll also stop trying to hide my needs from God and will be more willing to open myself to Him. One of our natural tendencies is to try to present the very best face possible to God—perhaps because of a hidden belief that if He ever *really* knew what we were like, He wouldn't listen to us at all. What a distorted view of the nature of God. First of all, He already knows everything about us. Second, He's already taken care of all of the things that defile us so that He can enjoy our presence, and so we can enjoy the privilege of walking and working with Him.

Maybe we should spend more of our time looking for our weaknesses than for our strengths. Those things that we call strengths actually may be our weaknesses because they prevent God from showing His glory in us. On the other hand, those things we overlook, hide, or ignore might just be the greatest opportunity we've ever had to experience the life of God and thus exhibit His glory to the world.

We're talking about confident praying. We can be absolutely confident when our prayers are for the purpose of glorifying His mercy. That glorifies His name. He is looking all over to find a place to reveal his name.

> For the eyes of the LORD range throughout the earth to strengthen those whose hearts are fully committed to him.[18]

The second phrase of the model prayer gives us another clue to confident praying: "Thy kingdom come, thy will be done." God is committed to establishing and enforcing His kingdom on earth. When our lives and prayers live up to that purpose, we are praying His will. Read on to see the value of living and praying with a "kingdom consciousness."

A NEW
WORLD ORDER

resident George Bush used a phrase several years ago, immediately after the demise of Communism in Europe, that made many political conservatives nervous. He spoke of a "new world order." I want to use that phrase to describe what God is doing in the earth. A new world order has been inaugurated in Jesus Christ. It is at work in the earth and it is destined to overcome everything that opposes it. It is so glorious that every person with the DNA to make a difference will be attracted to it. Participation in its fulfillment makes any sacrifice worthwhile.

The biblical phrase that describes this new world order is the "kingdom of God," or the "kingdom of heaven." It's little more than a stock phrase in some religious circles. It's mentioned often, understood little, and experienced even less. Many Christians identify the kingdom of God with the church or with political involvement by people of faith. But God's kingdom is much bigger than any of that. It reveals the nature of the King, permeates and transforms all of society, and transcends generations. God is up to something big in His kingdom. We need to know what it is and how to get in on it.

The King Now Reigns

Every kingdom must have a king, and this one does. Jesus has already begun His reign. We will miss the glory of God's kingdom if we relegate it entirely to the future. As we read Jesus' parables about the kingdom, we find some of them emphasizing how it will be in the future. But many of them emphasize the way the kingdom is expressed now—before Jesus' return in the end. If we learn about the present aspects of the kingdom we can begin participating in it today. Jesus is already on His throne, and His administration of all things has already begun.

In the Old Testament God had a series of kings. David's reign represented the high-water mark of Israel's monarchy, and prophecies to Israel and Judah after David's kingship always focused on restoring his throne. God had promised David that one of his descendants would always sit on the throne of God's kingdom. So Israel looked for years for a descendant of David to fulfill those prophecies. Jesus came to fulfill them all, and His reign represents God's faithfulness to His promises.

In Acts, chapter 2, we find out that Jesus' reign is not only in the future. On the Day of Pentecost those who had followed Jesus burst out of an upper room full of the Holy Spirit's power and speaking languages they had never learned. The crowd tried to figure out what was going on. They reasoned that these followers must be drunk. The Holy Spirit inspired Peter to respond, and we can read that response in verses 14 through 39. Part of it refers to David:

> "Brothers, I can tell you confidently that the patriarch David died and was buried, and his tomb is here to this day. But he was a prophet and knew that God had promised him on oath that he would place one of his descendants on his throne. Seeing what was ahead, he spoke of the resurrection of the Christ, that he was not abandoned to the grave, nor did his body see decay. God has raised this Jesus to life, and we are all witnesses of the fact. Exalted to the right hand of God, he has received from the Father the promised Holy Spirit and has poured out what you now see and hear. For David did not ascend to heaven, and yet he said,
>
> "'The Lord said to my Lord: "Sit at my right hand until I make your enemies a footstool for your feet."'
>
> "Therefore let all Israel be assured of this: God has made this Jesus, whom you crucified, both Lord and Christ."[1]

Verse 37 says that the crowd was cut to the heart by what Peter said. What was it that so convicted them? They had seen the effect of ordinary men filled with the Holy Spirit, and Peter's explanation of those things climaxed with the establishment of David's throne through Jesus Christ. The same man who had been crucified in that same city only weeks before rose from the dead, ascended, and sat on the throne of heaven. Everything they were hearing and seeing attested to the fact that Jesus

Christ was the King the Jewish people had been expecting for centuries. And they had crucified Him. Instead of welcoming the advent of God's kingdom on earth, they had resisted and opposed it.

Sadly, many of us have missed the significance of Jesus' present reign. When we speak of Jesus as King, we do so in a passive and detached way. But the fact of Jesus' reign changes everything about everything. I am disturbed when I hear believers speak of Satan's activity as if it were any match for Jesus' kingdom. I'm not nearly as impressed with the devil's power and strategy as I am with Jesus' kingdom. He is King of those who recognize Him and of those who do not. And we who know Him must live in the glorious light of that reality.

There has been a revolution in the heavenlies, and Jesus Christ occupies the throne.[2] Satan has been cast down from his pretentious place. People on earth are in league with one or the other. Those of us who think we rule our own lives are the unwitting cohorts of darkness. Those of us who recognize and celebrate the rule of Christ can cooperate with light and life. There is no middle ground of non-aligned humanity.

The Domain Is on the Earth

Knowing that there is such a King as Jesus, our minds easily move to the next question: Where does He want to rule? Of course, He rules from heaven. He is seated at the right hand of the Father. But the project He is most interested in has Him ruling in the earth. His last statement about this makes it clear:

Then Jesus came to them and said, "All authority in heaven and on earth has been given to me. Therefore go and make disciples of all nations, baptizing them in the name of the Father and of the Son and of the Holy Spirit, and teaching them to obey everything I have commanded you. And surely I am with you always, to the very end of the age."[3]

We call this passage the great commission. And its greatness is enhanced when we see it in the context of God's revelation. It is the last and most complete restatement of the commission God has given us repeatedly since the first chapter of Genesis.

When God created the first man and woman, He assigned them the task of filling the earth and subduing it. He wanted His highest creation to represent His interests on the earth and rule as His vice regent. When Adam and Eve sinned, they lost their authority to fulfill their mandate from God. God never lost any of His authority—but humanity did. But when Jesus came to the earth as the Son of Man, He regained that authority for us. Along with His sacrifice for our sin, He also restored to us the authority God has always wanted for us in the earth.

Contrary to the sentiment of many Christians, the earth is important to God. It is more than the ol' mudball we live upon until Jesus returns. Many of us have misapplied biblical teaching about the eventual destruction of the earth by fire. We have concluded that since nothing here is permanent, then nothing we do here is really important. We justify running up our debts and wasting natural resources by saying that the Antichrist and his followers will have to sort it all out. But the Bible teaches that what we are doing now on earth has eternal significance for our own relationship with God and participation in His kingdom. A central teaching of Scripture is that the way we handle things here determines whether we increase or diminish in authority for eternity.

Too many Christians are counting on death to make them immediately mature. Their doctrine of eternality is flawed. They've seen the wonderful promises that Jesus will glorify us after death and come to the wrong conclusions. We cannot live sloppy, irresponsible lives here and now without eternal consequences. Sin and tears will be wiped away in heaven. But our stewardship here and now has implications even in eternity—so the earth and how we use it is very important.[4]

The amazing implication of Jesus' teaching is that if we're willing to subject ourselves to His kingdom, we can rule the earth with Him. His character will govern ours and our lives will produce the fruit He desires. By submitting to His authority, we can learn to exercise it in our arenas of responsibility. When Jesus was here on earth, He demonstrated the superiority of His kingdom to every natural power. He healed sickness, cast out demons, raised the dead, calmed storms, and multiplied food. And that superior kingdom is the one we receive when we cooperate with Jesus.

Jesus also lived His life in the revelational power of God's kingdom. He had wisdom, knowledge, and insight from God beyond natural observation. And those abilities have been given to us in the form of spiritual gifts. By receiving and responding to them, we can communicate with God and know how to exercise authority for His ends. When the Christians who believe in these gifts move them beyond their church meetings and into the marketplaces and neighborhoods, something powerful will happen. The authority of Jesus over the earth will be made visible and tangible.

The responsibility to permeate and influence every aspect of society with kingdom truth and power is ours. And with obedience comes fulfillment. The cure for lackadaisical, passionless, and purposeless Christians lies here. As long as our concept of being a Christian is limited to attending church, serving on a board or committee, giving a little money, and following a few rules, we are doomed to boredom at best.

A younger generation sees us going through these motions and calling it Christianity. Is it any wonder they aren't interested? They don't like tedium any better than we do. We are losing a generation because of the distorted picture we're giving them. But if we lived as if we believed Jesus is destined to rule the earth as completely as He rules heaven, things would be different. Every generation would love to sign on to a project that is destined to succeed.

Ruling through His Word

To get at this subject of the kingdom as a new world order, we need to return to some essential truths. If we know there is a King (Jesus) and a domain (the earth), one question remains: how does this King rule His domain? Does He use military might or strategically placed leaders? No. Jesus rules His kingdom through His word. So when Jesus wanted to teach about His kingdom in Matthew 13, He gave His disciples parables about the word of God.

> Then he told them many things in parables, saying: "A farmer went out to sow his seed. As he was scattering the seed, some fell along the path, and the birds came and ate it up. Some fell on rocky places, where it did not have much soil. It sprang up quickly, because the soil was shallow. But when the sun came up, the plants were scorched, and they withered because they had no root. Other seed fell among thorns, which grew up and choked the plants. Still other seed fell on good soil, where it produced a crop—a hundred, sixty or thirty times what was sown. He who has ears, let him hear."[5]

This parable is about a farmer who went into his fields to sow. By hand he scattered seed all over the ground and the seed fell on different kinds of soil. Some seed fell on hard ground, some on rocky soil. Some fell on soil polluted with weeds and thorns. The rest fell on good, fertile soil. Those soils received the same seed but produced very different results.

When the disciples asked Jesus to explain what the story meant, He told them they must understand this one if they hoped to grasp any other teaching about the kingdom. According to Jesus, this story has truth so seminal and germane that if we fail to grasp it we will miss the kingdom entirely.

The central idea of the parable of the sower is clear because Jesus explained it in detail. The issue in focus is the heart's response to God's word. The seed in the story represents the word of God. The soils represent different states of the human heart in terms of their response to that word.

Response Determines Destiny

In practical terms, this parable teaches us that our response to the word of the kingdom determines our destiny. All the folk who are fretting and asking about their life purpose, looking for meaning, really are looking for what only God's word can provide. All individuals in every generation cooperate in their own destiny by their response to God's word.

The word of God can be defined simply as reality according to God's definition. It includes a Christian worldview. It allows God His prerogative of saying what truth is, what is right and wrong. By submitting to God's truth, we can become incarnations of it, the wheat that grows up from the seed. In the second parable of Matthew 13, Jesus describes the children of His kingdom as wheat and those who don't receive His kingdom as tares. It is as if the seed of the first parable has produced the crop of the second. God wants us to become mature expressions of His truth.

Overcoming the Obstacles

The challenges to receiving and practicing God's truth are the same in every generation. We need to look at this familiar story to find the possible range of responses and what contributes to them. Some people study this passage to determine which of the soils represent those who are "saved" and those who are not. But I don't think that is Jesus' purpose here. He wants to focus our attention on our own responses to truth. We who are saved can easily fall into the poor patterns described in the first three soils. So this parable is a warning to us to keep our hearts responsive.

THE HARD HEART

The first response Jesus describes in this parable is that of the hard heart. It has no place for God's opinions or definitions. It refuses to recognize God's right to define terms, set boundaries, and rule over all things. Even a believer's heart can be hard in some areas of life. Wherever one fails to submit to God's rule, another authority establishes itself. And that rule will cause disruption, confusion, and frustration. Eventually it will wreak destruction.

Many who reject God's sovereignty simply elevate their own values, their own independence, and their own individuality above God. These are the people who have replaced God's truth with their own opinions. They are often heard to say, "That's the way I see it," as if that should settle the matter for all time.

Jesus tells us what happens to the word of God in a hard heart. It is stolen away by the devil. It interests me to talk to people who have no concept of their mortality or eternity. They don't seem to give any thought at all to their inevitable death and what happens after that. It amazes me that anyone could live life oblivious to such an important issue. The only explanation I can come up with is that they have rejected God's truth and the devil has stolen it away. What's left is a superficial understanding of the most important issues of life. According to the Bible, the gospel is hidden to them because the god of this world has made them blind.[6]

We can harden our hearts in any area of life. When God brings His kingdom and its truth to bear in some aspect of our lives, we can refuse it or receive it. We usually try to put it off until another time, but that's not a viable option. It amounts to the same thing as refusing. When a king speaks, his subjects either obey or rebel. And those who insolently ignore this King find His truth stolen and often replaced with a counterfeit. They sometimes come back later to embrace God's truth, but it has been perverted. Those who choose to "obey" God on their own terms follow many heresies and cults. Deception is the penalty of rejecting truth.

THE SHALLOW HEART

Another response to the seed of the word comes from the shallow heart. It receives the word immediately, but superficially. Jesus compared it to a shallow layer of topsoil covering rock. The seeds can germinate, but their roots can't go down. So as soon as the midday sun bears down, the plant withers and dies. In the same way, many people hear the word of the kingdom and think it sounds great. They set out to live according to what they've heard. But as soon as persecution arises, their enthusiasm for truth withers away.

Jesus had lots of these folk in His crowds. They were impressed that He did miracles and taught wisdom, so they followed Him. Yet when difficulty came because of those very miracles and teachings, they fell away. In the case of the man who'd been born blind, which we mentioned in chapter 3, his parents acknowledged the miracle and spoke well of Jesus. But when the Pharisees made an issue of it, those parents chose to remain in the synagogue rather than to follow the Messiah.

Several years ago I visited the nation of Zaire (now the Democratic Republic of the Congo) and had a meeting with its longtime president. We shared the gospel with him and he assured us that he believed in Jesus. But it was evident then and later that what he had done was add Jesus to the witchcraft and superstition of his heritage. He didn't want to reject Jesus. Neither did he want to risk offending others. Sadly, he died recently in disgrace.

Many people want enough of the gospel to assure their place in heaven. They treat it as an insurance policy. They join a church and go through whatever procedure their church requires of them. But when they learn that the kingdom means submitting every part of life to the King, they balk. For fear of becoming imbalanced and radical, they back away.

Some of these are the politically correct who won't stand up for God's definition of the family. They urge us to be inclusive to gays and lesbians who want to redefine the family in terms that will suit their choices. The politically correct choose a humanist ethic over biblical teaching because it is socially less difficult.

Some cringe when we mention that education is primarily the responsibility of families assisted by their churches, and not the civil government's responsibility. Is it possible that loyalty to government-controlled schools is based more on sentimentality and irresponsibility than godly wisdom? I was educated through the secondary level in public schools. There wasn't much of an option. I greatly appreciate the committed teachers and administrators who sacrificed for my benefit.

For decades the values of a biblical worldview permeated the educational system—but that has changed. Our culture has moved to a post-Christian worldview. Its government-sponsored educational philosophy is in direct contradiction to the biblical basis of truth as we know it. If we embrace the kingdom of God, we must rethink our approach to education. It will be costly. But it is even more costly to ignore God's order.

Shallow hearts tend to reject the idea that God has established spheres of authority that must respect each other. Self-government, family government, church government, and civil government all cover their areas with divinely ordered authority. When they cross the boundaries between them, conflicts arise.

Americans have been told, "It's the economy, stupid!" And many have believed it. But in truth it's the kingdom that matters. Economies fail when they aren't founded in that kingdom. In other words, "It's the kingdom, you wise ones!"

We may think this part of the parable of the various soils doesn't apply to us "deeper" Christians. Because we have received much of the word of God, we can quote the Scriptures, and we know we're going to heaven, we consider ourselves beyond such shallowness. But if our lives never create conflict with the world around us, we may be deceiving ourselves. We may be under the delusion that the American dream is the same as biblical Christianity.

THE AMERICAN DREAM

In his excellent book *Nine Great American Myths,*[7] Pat Appel points out our tendency to identify American ideals with biblical Christianity. I agree with his thesis that we sometimes fight for American values against the best interests of God's kingdom. I consider myself patriotic. When Old Glory is raised I still get choked up. But I am convinced that Americanism is not Christianity. In recent years, when we exported what we call Christian faith to other nations, it didn't work. I have heard missionaries in Asia, South America, and Eastern Europe say they have been told our gospel was not wanted or needed.

Appel quotes from U.S. Senator Mark Hatfield's remarks at a National Prayer Breakfast in 1973:

> Let us be aware of the real danger of misplaced allegiance, if not outright idolatry, to the extent we fail to distinguish between the god of the American civil religion and the God who reveals himself in the Holy Scriptures and in Jesus Christ. If we as leaders appeal to the god of civil religion our faith is in a small and exclusive deity. A loyal spiritual advisor to power and prestige. A defender of only the American nation. The object of a national

folk religion devoid of moral content. But if we pray to the biblical God of justice and righteousness we fall under God's judgment for calling upon his name but failing to obey his commands.[8]

I'm concerned that the senator's diagnosis is uncomfortably accurate. What functions under the guise of Christianity in our nation is little more than civil religion. One of its cardinal doctrines is egalitarianism, the idea that all distinction should be abolished so that all people will be considered equal in every way. The Bible teaches that every person, because he or she is created in God's image, has equal value. But equal value does not translate into equal ability.

Anyone who doubts that we are not equally endowed should pay more attention to obvious realities. Try competing in baseball with any major league player, or match voices with a regular from the Metropolitan Opera. What began in America as a biblically based insistence on the equality of every person before the law has permuted into something quite different. It has now become controversial even to suggest that men and women have different capacities. In addition, followers have lost respect for leaders. To distinguish between leaders and followers is politically incorrect. It even seems un-American to speak against such ideas. But it is not unbiblical.

INDIVIDUALISM

Appel pointed out another earmark of Americanism—our regard for individualism.[9] One of our national heroes is the late John Wayne. I, too, am a fan of his movies, but the type of character he portrayed is not my ideal. He presented the aloof and independent loner. He added to the mythology of the self-made man. In fact, genuine Christianity knows nothing of an individual Christian outside of the community of faith. Everyone who comes to faith in Christ enters the fellowship of all other believers. We are part of a family, a nation, and a tradition that forms and equips us.

Christians in community understand that their spiritual gifts have value only as they cooperate with those of other believers. They honor the history of the church as deeply as they anticipate her destiny. Personal religious experience finds its counterpart in shared tradition and cooperation. American Christianity is afflicted with many forms of unhealthy individualism.

Ironically, our commitment to individualism leads us down a road to conformity. Vance Packard, in his 1957 book *The Hidden Persuaders*,[10] stated that except for those living at that time behind the Iron Curtain, Americans were the most manipulated people in the world.

Large-scale efforts are being made, often with impressive success, to channel our unthinking habits, our purchasing decisions, and our thought processes by the use of insights gleaned from psychiatry and the social sciences. Whether we are thought of as consumers or citizens, hidden persuaders are at work trying to invade the privacy of our minds.

When we consider ourselves disconnected individuals, we are cut off from the defining traditions of the past. We have no absolutes and no source of affirmation. Lacking this basic psychological component, we seek it elsewhere, usually among our contemporaries. Of course, they are mostly involved in the same search and struggle as we are, so we all become products of peer pressure. We are like the young people we chuckle about who insist they are making their own decisions while they wear the same clothes, earrings, and hairstyles.

This misconstrued individuality makes us vulnerable to the conforming pressure of the culture. As a result, those with a little bit of knowledge in social sciences and psychology manipulate the rest of us. Even Christians who profess to be guided by the Bible may be governed more than they know by Madison Avenue salesmanship. Our "independence" has made us just like those around us, but we sell it as part of our gospel.

RELATIVISM

Another ingredient of American values, along with egalitarianism and individualism, is relativism. In this country, we make our own decisions and choose our own values. And every set of values is equally valid. For instance, the right to dissent is considered a part of our national birthright. What should have been a blessing that ensures freedom against oppressive government has become a curse of dissension. We believe that if we don't agree, neither should we cooperate or even participate.

I see this played out in churches all across the United States. Members who disagree with the pastor or other leaders of a church on policy or programs feels it's their right to leave. They don't talk to the people who made the decision. They don't offer to help solve the problem. They simply find a church down the road that looks more like their ideal. We seem to put no value on the integrity of relationships within churches.

Shallow-hearted people will not survive these American myths with their faith intact. Only the word of the kingdom is strong enough to withstand deeply ingrained cultural values like these. Most of us need to do periodic checkups to see if we are living more American than Christian. The report from that evaluation may answer why we have so little purpose and passion and so much frustration.

THE CROWDED HEART

Some hearts receive the word of God but find it crowded out later by other concerns. This is the crowded heart. Jesus compared it to soil that has the seeds of weeds in it. After the plant seed has produced its crop, the weeds take over and choke out the good produce. Jesus identifies the weeds as "the worries of this life and the deceitfulness of wealth."[11] I think this kind of heart prevails in our generation. We have been duped by the deceitfulness of riches. We were promised that wealth would give us options and freedom. But the wealth we've managed to obtain has instead given rise to greed. Now we spend much of our time and energy protecting our assets instead of exercising our options.

People still become offended when churches talk about money and possessions. They leave churches huffing, "All they ever talk about is money." Of course Jesus would have offended these folks, too. He spoke of possessions more often than He did of heaven and hell. But when people have been confused by wealth's deception, they act this way. The word of God has been choked out by this deception. These people are looking for a form of Christianity that conforms to Americanism's emphasis on economic prosperity.

There is a segment of Christian ministry so focused on prosperity that it is identified with cars, jewelry, money, and other markers of wealth. Unbelievers mock us for it. It seems to offer the best of both worlds, comfort both now and later. But in fact, it poisons the essence of God's kingdom, which emphasizes permeating the world with the truth of God's sacrificial and self-giving love.

I know fathers who have taught their sons to give themselves completely in their early years to making money on the job. They admit that young fathers may miss out on a lot of their children's activities and important moments of growth. But, they reason, later that father will have the financial means to do more for his kids. Abiding by such counsel, many men have lost wives, children, health, and personal integrity for the sake of a lie. It can never really succeed because it runs counter to God's kingdom and truth.

In Jesus' parable of the sower, only one kind of heart is commended. That is the productive heart. When we hear and practice the word of God, our hearts produce a great harvest, just as fertile and plowed soil will turn seed into crop. Jesus spoke of land that would produce thirty, sixty, or even one hundred times what was planted.

Someone might look here and see a problem. If only one quarter of the ground produces fruit, those aren't good odds. But in Jesus' day farmers considered an increase of five to ten times good. Jesus might have spoken of a harvest ten times greater than the amount of seed sown. But instead He suggested an increase of thirty to one hundred times. In other words, the hearts that do produce can produce a lot. When the word is received, the return is not mediocre, but abundant.

A Kingdom on the Rise

In Jesus' parables about the kingdom there is a consistent theme. When He speaks of the mustard seed, He emphasizes how small it is when it begins and how large its bush becomes. The yeast hidden in a lump of dough begins small and influences the whole loaf. According to Jesus, the kingdom of God is a growing concern. It's already big, but it's also on the rise. Those who invest in it will come out way ahead.

God's new world order is destined to affect all creation. We are not a few struggling refugees waiting to be released from our camps. We are those who have received the word, applied it to every area of life, and begun to practice its implications. We are leavening the whole world with the truth that has captured our hearts. Ultimately, what we have believed will permeate and transform all that is.

God is trying to get our attention through instability in our society. He wants us to ask Him for His new world order. Political processes alone will never change a society, but when the kingdom of God is enforced, everything changes. When His people recognize the privilege and joy of cooperating with His reign, things will start to change dramatically. Love, servanthood, and faithfulness to God's word will win the day in God's time. His kingdom is destined to prevail.

Every person must rethink his or her place in this kingdom. We must examine our hearts for our response to God's truth. Are we adjusting our lives to His definitions of reality? Are we part of His new world order? Or are we abiding by Americanism in its garb of civil religion? The answers to these questions determine whether we welcome or dread the inevitable victory of the kingdom of God.

Father, give us eyes to see the kingdom. You said except a man be born again he cannot even see the kingdom of God. Lord, if anyone reading this is not born again I pray that today You would convict his or her heart. You have made Jesus king, and if we don't submit to His kingship we are eternally doomed. And I also pray for those of us who have been born again, but have rejected your word in some way. Show us where we have done this so that we can come back in repentance and become loyal subjects to the King who deserves to rule in this world. So let your kingdom come. Let your will be done on earth as it is being done in heaven. We pray in His name. Amen.

CHAPTER SEVEN

PRAYING
WITH HOPE

Now faith is being sure of what we hope for and
certain of what we do not see.

HEBREWS 11:1

S ome would have us believe that the influence of the kingdom of God
is diminishing and that God's plan is for the children of the kingdom to be defeated, then ultimately rescued by the Second Coming of
Jesus. If that's true, then praying with hope is difficult. Our prayers
would be limited to the needs of spiritual refugees surrounded by the
conquering armies of Satan and for the few that we might evangelize to
our camp. Maybe comprehensive, confident prayer has been hindered by
an adopted ideology that doesn't expect God's plan through His people
to succeed.

Is it possible that our neglect of the present reality of the kingdom
of God has crippled our prayers and, thus, our lives? There have been

two major mistakes in viewing the kingdom in recent history. First, we tend to think of the kingdom in future tense. Obviously, there is a future element to the kingdom Jesus announced while on earth, but it can't all be relegated to the future. To do so diminishes the power of the Cross that defeats the forces of the kingdom of darkness now. If the gospel of the Cross and resurrection can't beat the powers of hell, then we have a defective gospel and little hope in our living and praying.

The other great mistake regarding the kingdom of God has been to identify it totally with the church. When the kingdom of God is seen as the church, we get some confusing messages. First of all, the church is a bride being prepared for her husband. The church is the agent of the kingdom and is the instrument through which the kingdom is demonstrated on the earth. But to identify the church totally with the kingdom leaves us viewing the kingdom only in ecclesiastical or institutional terms, rather than as the permeating government and reality of God.

A Model of the Kingdom

Since we are to pray, "Thy kingdom come. Thy will be done, on earth as it is in heaven," we need some kind of model to know what that looks like. What does "Thy kingdom" look like on earth? Since Jesus is the kingdom of God personalized, we can safely say that His life on earth is what we are praying will be duplicated in all His disciples. Now *there's* some hope. Think of it! Thousands of disciples all over the world affecting their societies the way Jesus did.

The kingdom of God has always been a source of hope for God's people. Since Daniel prophesied that an eternal kingdom would be established at a specific time in history, and that it would crush and destroy opposing kingdoms, the people of God have hoped for that kingdom.[1] When John the Baptist came forth four hundred years after the last prophetic word in the Old Testament was recorded, he announced that the kingdom of God was at hand.[2] Then Jesus started His ministry and announced at the outset that the kingdom of God was near, meaning that it was accessible.[3] In His most comprehensive sermon, He described the life of one who embodied the kingdom of God.[4] (It is in that sermon that He gave us our key instruction on prayer and told us to pray, "Thy kingdom come. Thy will be done, on earth as it is in heaven.")

In the gospels, we see the kingdom incarnate, living life on earth, as it should be done. It is superior to nature (He calmed the wind and waves), to sin (He forgave sin), to disease (He healed the sick), to demons (He cast them out), and to death (He raised the dead and He Himself was resurrected from substitutionary death on the cross).

In the book of Acts, we see the power of that life being transferred to the disciples. They began to affect their world just as Jesus had predicted: "I tell you the truth, anyone who has faith in me will do what I have been doing. He will do even greater things than these, because I am going to the Father."[5]

Miracles that accompany these disciples are normal expressions of God's kingdom. Peter has a new revelation through a vision and breaks the barrier between Jews and Gentiles by giving the gospel to Cornelius.

Philip preaches the kingdom in Samaria and great miracles accompany his ministry. He himself is given instruction by an angel to go to the desert to meet with the Ethiopian authority, and as a result the gospel is given to Africa. Paul preaches the gospel of the kingdom and affects the known world. Our last account of Paul finds him in private quarters under house arrest in Rome. What is he doing? Preaching and teaching about the kingdom of God.[6]

Hope: Foundation of Faith

Just how important is hope? It is the foundation of faith. Without it no one can please God.

> Now faith is being sure of what we hope for and certain of what we do not see....And without faith it is impossible to please God, because anyone who comes to him must believe that he exists and that he rewards those who earnestly seek him.[7]

> Hope is essential for successfully confronting the obstacles of life.

> And hope does not disappoint us, because God has poured out his love into our hearts by the Holy Spirit, whom he has given us.[8]

> Since it is so important, our enemy Satan seeks to destroy our hope. It's no surprise that hopelessness is at the heart of all defeat and bondage.

And it's no wonder that so many theories abound on the effectiveness and final outcome of God's plan for us on earth. Elaborate schemes have been concocted to explain how God is going to save face when His plan for us to subdue the earth fails. But maybe we shouldn't give up yet. What did Jesus actually teach us about the kingdom?

Hope and the Parables of Jesus

The essential teaching of Jesus in His parables fosters the hope that turns to faith. Those parables that speak of the future aspect of the kingdom emphasize our accountable stewardship.[9] We are expected to be faithful to His commission until the end. Any theory or scheme that causes us to hesitate in our faithfulness in managing the earth under His control is faulty. Jesus made it clear in Matthew 24 that no one would know the time of His coming. He also made it clear that we are not to spend our time trying to figure that out, but rather are to spend our time fulfilling His last commission.

I grew up on a farm. I can remember many days spent in the field with a hoe in my hand. It was my job to eliminate the grass and weeds from the planted crop. Many times the task seemed so daunting that I found myself leaning on my hoe, wishing for the second coming of the Lord—or at least the coming of my dad to say, "You don't have to do this anymore." Neither Jesus nor my dad ever came to rescue me. Actually, what brought me the greatest sense of fulfillment was refusing to lean on the hoe and instead using it to do what I had been commanded already. There is joy in getting the job done.

TWO COMMISSIONS

God has given to us essentially two commissions. In the first, we are told to subdue the earth under His guidance.[10] We have been given both the ability and responsibility to do just that. With the fall of man our capacity to do this was perverted. Humanity, being separated from God, didn't know how to rule the earth in a way consistent with God's life and character. So we began to abuse ourselves, our neighbors, and the earth. Jesus came to reestablish our ability to do what we were originally commissioned to do. He showed us, while He was on earth, how to rule the earth under God's control. Then He gave to us His very life so that we could do the same as He had done.

When Jesus left, He gave to His disciples the second commission, which was to make disciples of Jesus Christ. It is only as men and women become disciples of Jesus that they regain the ability to subdue the earth under His control. Like Adam and Eve, we have been given our own specific garden. We are to take authority and responsibility for our garden and rule it according to His kingdom. When that is done, the earth will be subdued the way God wants it done.

If we as disciples would take seriously the command to bring the garden of our own personal life, our family, our church, our community, and our country under the rule of God, then the effect on our lives would be dramatic. We would truly be fulfilling our destiny of being the salt of the earth and the light of the world.

This is not an undoable task. It is not my responsibility to change the world, but it is my responsibility to bring my world under the domain of the kingdom of God. If I bring my garden under the kingdom of God and you bring your garden under the kingdom of God and we make disciples of other people, teaching them how to bring their gardens under the kingdom of God, then pretty soon there are lots of gardens under the kingdom of God—and this affects society.

Some of the disciples are in the garden of politics, while others are in the garden of education and still others are in the garden of technology. Some are in the garden of the marketplace. Some are in the garden of ecclesiology, while others are in the garden of the science lab. All of these areas need the infusion of the kingdom of God in order to work properly. To withdraw from any one of these spheres and simply drop back into the refugee camp of those fearful of the dark, perverse world is to adopt an attitude of irresponsibility. It flies in the face of all that Jesus taught in His parables about the culmination of the kingdom.

PARABLE OF THE SOWER

The other parables that speak of the present reality of the kingdom give us a ground of hope and faith. First, Jesus deals with the parable of the sower, which we discussed earlier. The emphasis of that parable is that the essence of the kingdom is the word of God. God is going to do what He does through His eternal word. His word will not be shaken, nor will it be destroyed. What He says is truth will prove, in the end, to be the only thing that stands. God is not worried about all the ideologies that rise up in the world because His word is ultimate reality.

Those who build on anything other than the word of God are building on sinking sand. Their houses will fall when the storms of life come.

Any of us who want to be sure that our prayers will be answered can endeavor to pray according to the Word of God. Many prayers recorded in the Scriptures can be adopted for our use in praying for the situations of our own lives. Many other promises of the Scriptures can be taken and used in prayer. When we pray the Word, we are praying the will of God; we can pray confidently. I have found it very helpful to use prayers in Scripture to help me pray. For instance, I use the prayers of Paul in Ephesians 1:15–23 and 3:14–21 to pray for believers. The Psalms are a great source for personal prayer. There seems to be a prayer for every mood I can get in. Proverbs gives great instruction to praying for wisdom.

PARABLE OF THE WHEAT AND TARES

The parable of the wheat and the tares essentially tells us that the greatest conflict that we will face on this earth is the counterfeit to real kingdom life. We have already dealt with this previously. Suffice it to say that, while on this earth, our greatest temptation will be to settle for something less than the real and be duped by the counterfeit. The hope that's given by this parable is that it is not left up to us to be the final judge between the wheat and the tares—that will be done by God and His angels. It is our privilege to walk in fellowship with Him and respond as He gives direction.

PARABLE OF THE MUSTARD SEED

The parable of the mustard seed is a great parable of hope. It teaches us that what starts off small and insignificant can end up large and useful. Jesus used the proverbial mustard seed to talk about the kingdom of God. In His day, when people wanted to say something was as small as possible, they would say that it was as small as a mustard seed. When Jesus told this story, I'm sure eyebrows were raised when He said the mustard seed became the largest plant in the garden. This would require a supernatural occurrence.

Some who come to the teachings of Jesus with a presupposition of pessimism have insisted that this parable is teaching about the unnatural growth of the false kingdom. I've found that to be an unsatisfactory interpretation for many reasons—primarily because Jesus says the "kingdom of heaven," not a false kingdom, is like this. I think Jesus is teaching that what began small and insignificant will finish being the most prominent and useful of everything that is planted in the earth.

We can see it already in that Jesus started off as an insignificant baby in an insignificant manger in an insignificant town. He lived what, to the eyes of some, was an insignificant life. Yet His life, death, burial, resurrection, and teachings have affected the whole world. When Jesus said that the mustard seed would grow up into the likeness of a tree, He was opening up all sorts of biblical allusions to the Jews who were listening to His words. Every Jew would have known that a tree giving shelter to the birds was a familiar Old Testament figure for a mighty kingdom giving shelter to the nations. [11]

PARABLE OF THE LEAVEN

In the parable of the leaven, Jesus encourages our hope through telling us about the unnoticed, permeating power of the kingdom. A surprising element of this parable is the amount of flour that the woman uses in the story. Instead of just taking enough flour for her own family, she instead takes enough for a large number of people. Jesus is saying that a little bit of yeast can permeate a whole lot more than we might have first thought. This leaven, as He says, permeates the whole lump of dough, therefore guaranteeing that it will get its job done before the end comes.

Again, some have interpreted this parable from the pessimistic side. They say that leaven is used in Scripture to refer to that which is evil, so this parable must be teaching about the permeating power of evil. But leaven can be used as a symbol of either evil or good. The context of the passage tells us which is intended. Jesus isn't talking about the *character* of the leaven here, but about its permeating nature. Many symbols in Scripture are used both for evil and good. For instance, the devil is referred to as a roaring lion in 1 Peter 5:8, yet Jesus is referred to as the lion of the tribe of Judah in Revelation 5:5.

A significant feature of the parable is that this little bit of leaven is *hidden* in the dough. It is unseen, unnoticed by anyone. The hiddenness of the gospel of the kingdom should not be mistaken for its absence.

Members of the early church evidently garnered hope from these teachings of Jesus, for they approached their world with an optimistic expectation for God's kingdom to win in every circumstance.[12] Though the early church was primarily made up of a ragtag, uneducated bunch, they permeated their known world and affected every aspect of society. The Roman Empire was unbelievably strong and would have seemed an insurmountable problem for that small band of believers. But Rome began to crumble under the weight of its own decadence. Members of the early church began to subdue the world around them. They built strong families and ministered to the sick and to the poor. They refused to become victims of their society. They worked hard at whatever they did, giving glory to God and becoming the best workmen on the job. They adopted babies that were left to die. They kept their own hearts pure and their own hopes high because they believed in the ultimate victory of the kingdom of God.

By the year 312 A.D., Constantine came to power and declared that Christianity was the state religion. This wasn't necessarily a good thing for Christianity as a whole—but it did reveal the fact that the Christian way of life had so permeated Roman society that it could be made a state religion without there being a major backlash.

Tertullian made a statement a hundred years earlier that had been dramatically fulfilled. He said, "We came on the scene only yesterday and already we fill all your institutions, your towns, walled cities, your fortresses, your senate, and your forum."[13] In a matter of three hundred years, that which had started off as an insignificant baby in an insignificant manger in an insignificant town had conquered the greatest empire of the world.

There are those who are ready to give up the fight and call for Jesus to come and rescue us from the terrible plight we're in. We must not lose sight of the leavening power of the gospel of the kingdom that continues to work, often unnoticed, yet able to permeate even the unyielding nature of the world. G. K. Chesterton has said, "At least five times, therefore, with the Arian and the Albigensian after the humanist skeptics, after Voltaire and after Darwin, the faith has in all appearance gone to the dogs. In each of those five cases, it was the dog that died."[14]

PARABLE OF THE GROWING SEED

Then there is Jesus' story of the growing seed. The farmer who plants a seed, goes to bed, gets up and goes to bed again, and so on until one day he finds that the seed has begun to produce—how, he doesn't know. This parable teaches us that there are some aspects of the kingdom of God that remain mysterious, that we cannot control.

This is to give us hope. There is built into the nature of God's word and His way a progression that produces life. We can neither totally explain it, nor can we program it. Many times, because our explanations and programs fail, we conclude that the kingdom of God isn't making progress. This parable tells us that it's all right to live with mystery, that we must live with patience. Though *we* can't make it happen, it will happen because God Himself is behind it.

PARABLES OF THE TREASURE IN THE FIELD AND THE PEARL OF GREAT PRICE

The parables of the treasure in the field and the pearl of great price show us that when the kingdom is seen properly, it's worth trading everything we have in order to get it. All of life in the kingdom can be described as a trade up. Repentance is no longer about giving up what we really want for what we need in order to get to heaven. Rather, it is a realization that the kingdom of heaven provides a life that is superior to any other form of life in the universe—and when seen properly, we will "with joy" give up everything we have in order to obtain it.

PARABLE OF THE DRAGNET

The parable of the dragnet teaches us that when the kingdom of God has done its final work, it will have reached every segment of society, every tribe, every nation, every corner of the earth. The net that Jesus described had in it every kind of fish. The kingdom will succeed. Every aspect of life will be permeated with the leavening power of the gospel of the kingdom. Every corner of the lake will be netted so that no one will be left out of the opportunity to participate in the kingdom of God.

We can see, as we look at Jesus' essential teachings about the kingdom, that all of them are to give us hope. None of them are designed to cause us to lean on our hoe or to retreat into our cave out of fear of the pervasive evil in the world. We must, and can, go forth with an optimistic attitude, fulfilling the mission that God has given to us. He wants us to subdue the earth under the kingdom of God. To do that we must make disciples of all the nations so that they'll know how to bring every aspect of life under that rule. So as we send up our incense, we are confident that God will answer with the thunder of His word, calling and equipping disciples to subdue the earth in His name.

CHAPTER EIGHT

THE REIGN
OF PEACE

Do not be anxious about anything, but in everything,
by prayer and petition, with thanksgiving, present your requests to God.
And the peace of God, which transcends all understanding,
will guard your hearts and your minds in Christ Jesus.

PHILIPPIANS 4:6–7

This well-known biblical injunction connects prayer and peace as indispensable to each other. Real prayer will ultimately produce peace. Peace is the atmosphere where prayer is most effective. Many have quoted Philippians 4:6–7 in times of turmoil, hoping for peace. That's a good first step, but to enjoy this kind of peace there's more required than quoting the verse.

A disease more serious than cancer prevails in today's world. It creates even more turmoil where it rages unchecked. But the good news is that this disease is curable. The name of the disease is chaos, the enemy of what the Bible calls peace.

In the biblical account of Creation we learn that the world was once formless and empty. But in the midst of that chaos where nothing was in order, God spoke His order into existence; cosmos came out of chaos. The world He has given us bears the beauty of intricate order. For those whose presuppositions allow it, every direction they look in Creation will amaze them and move them to worship the God who has created it. The celestial constellation and the terrestrial anthill alike reveal a God of order.

The eternal principle of God's order and peace affects our inner lives, our families, our churches, and our civil governments. The essential difference between order and disorder, or between cosmos and chaos, in any area of life is one thing only: the presence of God's word.

He sent forth his word and healed them.[1]

That is His way of doing it. He created the world by His word and He sustains everything in it by the same means.

No time in history has demonstrated the lack of peace in people's hearts more than our own. I sometimes conduct informal surveys asking people about their felt needs. Everywhere I go I find people worried, anxious, and confused. And their bodies bear the burden in ulcers, stress, and sicknesses. A quick way to make a fortune today is to publish a book that purports to solve the problem of stress. Reconciliation between races, denominations, and social classes has become a common theme. But if we seek peace apart from God's order, our well-intended attempts at bridging the gaps in society will continue to frustrate us.

Philippians, chapter 4, contains some of the best instruction in all the Word of God about a life of true peace and how it relates to prayer. We tend to especially like verse 7: "And the peace of God, which transcends all understanding, will guard your hearts and your minds in Christ Jesus." Likewise, verse 9 says, "And the God of peace will be with you." But too often we ignore the context of those promises and the principles that support them. The whole passage from verse 4 to verse 9 tells us how to bring our lives under the rule of Jesus Christ. Before we look at them in detail, we should learn more about the idea of peace in the Bible.

Liberation Rather than Restriction

Many people misunderstand the nature of genuine peace because they miss the essence of Jesus' ministry. In Luke 4, Jesus defined His mission in life in the words of the Old Testament prophet Isaiah. Jesus Christ is eternal truth in human form, so His testimony about anything is pretty important. At the beginning of His earthly public ministry, Jesus went to the synagogue in His hometown. He read that day's Scripture:

"The Spirit of the Lord is on me, because he has anointed me
to preach good news to the poor. He has sent me to proclaim

freedom for the prisoners and recovery of sight for the blind, to release the oppressed, to proclaim the year of the Lord's favor."[2]

In verse 21, Jesus claimed this passage as His mission statement. There is one obvious link in the various aspects of His ministry: The sole purpose of Jesus' work and words was to liberate people. Whether they were poor, brokenhearted, captive, or blind, Jesus' agenda was to set them free from the bondage and oppression in which He found them. Nothing He says here leads us to believe He wants to restrict us from anything. If we read the Gospels in light of this mission, we will understand them correctly.

Many Christians trying hard to do it right have turned Jesus' words into another set of lifeless commands. I've heard people explain the Sermon on the Mount that way. They make it all so restrictive and difficult. For instance, in that sermon Jesus said that if a man slaps me on the cheek, I am to turn the other cheek. And if a man takes away my coat, I am to offer him my sweater, too. If a man forces me to carry his load for a mile, I am to volunteer for another mile. Jesus said that anger is as serious as murder and that lust is as despicable as adultery.

All that sounds very stringent to us. But if we read the same words in the light of Jesus' stated purpose, they become something very different. Jesus is not telling us such counter-intuitive things to restrict us. He wants to liberate us from selfishness, from vain pride, from resentment, from anger, and from lust. Every command of God serves as a key to unlock another manacle from our limbs.

It makes no sense to fight against these commands. But we do it because we see them as restrictions instead of emancipation. We think we want to be free to do whatever we want. But what we really desire, as believers, is to have our "wanters" transformed to conform to God's ways. Bondage to our old desires can be replaced by the liberty to yield to the commands of Jesus and to the Spirit He has put within us. Together they release us to experience the universe with minimum restrictions.

The kingdom of God is the way God does things where His authority is recognized. In that kingdom, government always precedes peace. In all our talk about peace, very little is said about the prerequisite of government. We are told that meditation will bring us peace. Or that we can find peace by being filled with the Holy Spirit. We hear that getting our lives aligned with right priorities will create calm. Any of these things might be part of a peaceful life, but God's peace always comes out of His government. Until we submit to God's kingdom, any peace we experience will be temporary and illusory.

That great passage in Isaiah, chapter 9, speaks of Jesus as the Prince of Peace, and in describing His reign it says,

Of the increase of his government and peace there will be no end.[3]

Notice how government and peace are connected. Without the righteous order of government, true peace is impossible. In our world, dominated as it is by subjectivity, we need to hear again this ancient truth. The peace we are looking for so desperately is found only by those submitted to God's government.

Self-Government

All government begins with self-government, which is the fruit of God's Spirit. When Jesus' words and works become the final authority in our lives, we can expect to experience peace. There is no end of Jesus' government and peace. So those who cooperate with His government enjoy His peace. One biblical proverb says, "When a man's ways are pleasing to the LORD, he makes even his enemies live at peace with him."[4] A man whose ways please God is a man with the self-control to live under God's government.

I recently conversed with a young woman who was terribly upset that her parents didn't acknowledge her as a Christian. They didn't want her influencing some younger family members. She accused her parents of being narrow minded. She told me, "I believe in God and Jesus and all that. But my concept of God is that he is good, not judgmental and harsh." She spoke glowingly of how she experienced God in the beauty of nature. I asked her, "How do you define goodness? When you say that God is good, what do you mean?" She answered, "Well, good things make me feel good and bad things make me feel bad."

I had to tell this young woman that I agreed with her folks. Based on what I'd heard, she was not a Christian. She certainly didn't have a biblical understanding of this basic issue. In her system she was god, because she determined for herself, based on her emotions and perceptions, what was good and evil. She had no concept of God defining those things for her by His word and works.

I'm amazed at how many people hang on to the idea that they are Christians when they believe pretty much the same thing this woman does. I wonder what some people mean when they claim to be Christians. Christian as opposed to communist? Christian rather than atheist? Genuine Christians seek the peace that passes understanding. And they find it in submitting to God's government in every area of their lives. That's self-government.

Gifts and Government

Part of the wonderful dignity of being created in God's image is our capacity to create. God has given us this gift, but our enemy wants to pervert it. In all of human history, where creativity has flourished the temptation to idolatry has followed. It was true in ancient Greece and in the Italian Renaissance. When a person is unusually gifted in the arts, those who appreciate that work often worship the artist. Instead of honoring the God who gave the gift, people fawn over the image-bearer.

God's purpose for giving us creative abilities is that we may use them to express His glory in the earth. No matter how cleverly it's expressed, perversion rejects the government of God. Today, those who want to express perversion with great creativity dominate the arts. From the most prestigious museums to top-forty songs, we find people being degraded in the name of creativity instead of God being honored. They are all forms of idolatry. If a person can oversee a great corporation we applaud him, no matter what that enterprise might be doing. If an author can use words to say things well, she is honored in spite of what she might be saying with those words. Our culture worships the creature rather than the Creator.

All the creativity God has given us must be submitted to the kingdom of God. Much more than unencumbered self-expression is at issue here. Creativity must align with destiny, and only God has a clear picture of any person's destiny. But if we create to honor and glorify and reveal God and His ways, we are on track. Whatever we create should lead others to the conclusion that the God who made us creative is worthy to be honored. Otherwise we use His gifts against Him.

The artisans who helped adorn the temple were talented people whose work was recognized as a gift from God. David was obviously a great musician and songwriter. This is not to suggest that only those who use their creativity in religious or "church" ways are righteous. A work doesn't have to have a cross engraved on it to be holy. But it should declare truth about God and His creation, rather than a lie.

Gifts to Manage

Besides giving us the capacity to create, God has also blessed each of us with gifts to manage for the sake of His kingdom. He expects us to use whatever talents, resources, and abilities He's put in our hands for His purposes. Each of us is building a city, either God's or our own. The great biblical example of the city of men is the story in Genesis 11 of the tower of Babel. Men set out to build a great tower that would reach up to God.

But their real agenda was to magnify human accomplishments. They had all they needed to complete the job because God had given it to them. But God didn't want it done, so He confused their language and made it impossible for them to cooperate.

This urge to build a city of man has been around since Adam and Eve left the Garden. We want to build life around what we want, what we value, and what pleases us. Today we describe it with the term humanism, but it is really the same old effort to build the city of man. God put us here to work on His city, not our own. He wants the earth to be like the order of heaven. Jesus told us to pray that way: "Your kingdom come, your will be done on earth as it is in heaven." All the gifts we have are supposed to be marshaled for that end. But we seem to think it's acceptable to use those gifts to build personal kingdoms.

Imagine a man hires you to build his house. He gives you several million dollars to build a magnificent residence. You have his authority to spend that money for tools, workers, and materials. He's given you all the resources you need to complete the job. If you take the money and build a house for yourself, you'll be in jail pretty soon. You'll be a thief.

Yet when God gave us the resources to build His city, He put us in exactly this position. He wants His order according to His word and for His glory in every endeavor of life. If we use what He has put in our hands to build our own empires, it doesn't matter that we try to justify it by sending some little bit of it to a ministry or church. The point is not what we do with the 10 percent but what we are doing with the 90 percent. If we aren't using it to establish and extend God's government, we are stealing.

There is no peace in such a life no matter how many Valium we take. A weekly session with a counselor won't undo the damage of trying to rob God. Peace isn't found on the therapist's couch, but at the King's throne. The choice between peace and chaos stands before us in the way we use God's gifts and our capacity for creativity. These are at the heart of self-government.

Family Peace

God has always intended for His government and peace to be established in the earth through families. His instructions and principles on family life are given to liberate us, not to restrict us. Anyone who sees them otherwise needs a change of mind.

God says that the husband is to be the lead servant at home. And in commanding it, God is trying to set us free at home. He wants every husband to experience the freedom of fulfilling the responsibility he is gifted to fulfill. God says that wives are to be covered, cared for, and served by their husbands. It's His way of setting wives free of the fear of abuse and not being appreciated that is deep in their souls. Our society resists God's ideas because it doesn't understand that the essence of leading is serving.

God also says that children must honor their parents. In our day dishonoring parents has become the norm. Our tendency to conform the gospel to psychology is more damaging to the family than any legislation we complain about. Too much effort has been expended trying to heal people by helping them blame their parents for their problems. Of course, where genuine pain and scars exist, they must be acknowledged.

It helps to identify pain in order to receive comfort and healing. But for individuals to use their parents' wrongs to justify their own is wrong and counterproductive. There is nothing new about the insight that parents mess up. And some of them mess up terribly. But nothing a parent has done releases children from a divine obligation to honor their parents.

Another Proverb says, "If a man curses his father or his mother, his lamp will be snuffed out in pitch darkness."[5] And in a list of a series of despicable characteristics is this: "There are those who curse their fathers and do not bless their mothers."[6] These words describe our generation. We minimize the importance of honoring parents. But when God established society with only ten phrases of instruction, one of the ten was the command to honor parents. And that command includes a promise of blessing for the son or daughter who will obey it.

People who have been deeply damaged by their parents find this hard to receive. I have been in personal ministry long enough to hear the wretched stories of many people who have been mistreated by their parents. I would not shame anyone who needs to go through an intensive process of recovery because of this mistreatment. But I am insisting that healing never comes through disobeying God's clear command to honor parents. We are connected to our parents whether we want to be or not. We cannot cut them off or ignore their influence on us. We must find ways to honor them.

If we are to have peaceful homes, we must find God's government in them. And the right relationships between husbands and wives and between children and parents are part of that government. If we are determined to submit to God's way, we will find a way to do it. And it will liberate us rather than limit us.

Church Peace

Many churches experience great turmoil because they reject God's order. Ephesians 4:11–13 describes His way of governing the church. But too few churches submit to it. There are five ministries that equip the saints for their multiplied ministries. The apostles, prophets, evangelists, pastors, and teachers are the lead servants to the rest of the church. But for years only one of the five has been allowed to function in most churches. Only pastors have been recognized as having authority to govern churches.

George Barna's research shows that less than 10 percent of evangelical pastors in the United States have leadership abilities.[7] Yet almost 100 percent of those pastors are expected to lead. As a result, both pastors and people are frustrated. Pastoring is among the vocations that lead the list of burnout victims. The average CEO in business handles three or four major responsibilities a week. But the average local church pastor handles ten to fifteen. No one can handle that load for long and prosper. Their relationships suffer. Their bodies break down. They burn out and quit.

The men leading most churches suffer the devastation of neglecting the team of leaders to which they are called. If they could be joined with the other four, perhaps things could be different. Until these other servants, too, are recognized by churches as leaders, not just speakers, the church will not be in God's order. God's government must mean more to us than denominations and traditions. His word establishes His government and His peace in the church.

Civil Peace

Whenever law does not align with justice, turmoil ensues. Americans have witnessed it in other nations for years. But lately it's happened in our own. Our laws have less and less in common with God's eternal justice, and all kinds of problems arise as a result. Tyranny creates turmoil. When one jurisdiction trespasses on the prerogatives of another, you have tyranny. History testifies to the pain and turmoil—crusades, inquisitions—caused when ecclesiastic and civil governments confuse their responsibilities.

As previously discussed, that's what we're seeing today in the educational system. God gave the responsibility for training children not to the civil authority, but to parents. The church is to assist the family in that endeavor. Parents, particularly fathers, are to teach their children. The church, which is the pillar and ground of the truth, is to equip and assist parents in their task. God holds parents accountable for the education of their children. Only the right order will establish genuine peace.

Welfare is another area of tyranny today. In God's kingdom, needy people have always been the responsibility of the family and church, rather than the civil government. Families are to care for their elderly parents and needy children. If they can't, then the church is to step in. Paul gave clear direction for Timothy to implement the order of God's government regarding those requiring help. The family was first respon-sible, and then the local assembly if there was no family.[8]

But we have participated in today's tyranny by yielding to it. It doesn't help to have good people in civil government if they are trying to manage a system that is inherently out of divine order. Godly civil servants will help civil government get out and stay out of areas God has not assigned it responsibility. To experience peace, every area of government and authority must align with God's plan.

Peace Maintains Order

We have seen that right government establishes genuine peace. But it is also true that internal peace maintains divine government. A passage in Colossians says, "Let the peace of Christ rule in your hearts."[9] The Greek word translated *rule* in this verse could also be rendered *umpire*. Chris-tians often need to rely on the internal peace of God to help them make important decisions. The absence or presence of peace becomes a factor, sometimes the only factor, in those decisions. It becomes the umpire. I've heard Christians justify leaving their wives by saying, "I've prayed about it and I have peace that this is the right thing to do." Others have said, "I'm going to put my money into this investment because I have peace about it."

I agree that God's peace acts as an umpire in the hearts of believers, but I am concerned that we may misunderstand the role of an umpire. An umpire in sports is the person responsible for enforcing the rules of the game on the field of play. He keeps order and peace by knowing all the rules and making decisions on the basis of those rules. He can't make up the rules as he goes along.

In baseball, one of the umpires stands directly behind the batter and catcher at home plate. The umpire must call every ball thrown by the pitcher to the plate either a ball or a strike. It is either inside or outside the strike zone. He cannot watch a head-high fastball come in and call it a strike simply because he *feels* like it's one. Neither can he call a ball when a pitch splits the plate belt-high on the batter. He is not making up the rules, but enforcing rules already established.

God's peace functions in our hearts in the same way. We cannot rely on peace to govern our hearts if we are ignorant of the rules. The umpire of peace must always agree with the rules of God's kingdom. Investment decisions, for instance, will never garner the peace of God unless they conform to biblical parameters for God's will and work. But if we seek God's peace without knowing God's rules, the peace we feel or don't feel is unreliable as a guide in decisions. A human conscience is easily seared. And perverted peace can lead one down a dangerous path.

Sometimes we mistake irresponsible relief for genuine peace. Things get tough and pressured, and instead of facing the problems, we take a vacation to the beach. Lying in the sun with our feet in the sand, we think, *Finally, I've got peace.* The problem isn't solved. God's way has not been sought or found. God's provision hasn't been revealed. But we think we have peace because we have avoided the pressure. This is peace without order. It is an umpire ignorant of the rulebook. It is not the government of God.

There are, of course, those who think that keeping the rules is the entire game. *Okay,* they say to themselves, *If I can just keep all the rules, I'll win the game.* But that is deception. In fact, far too many of these folks never get out of the stands and play the game. Yet they consider themselves experts on the rules. They have an abundance of spiritual pride in their knowledge of Christianity. They look down on players who break the rules. But the guy breaking the rules while he tries to play the game is better off than the one in the stands reading the rulebook. The umpire can work with the player to correct him and make him a better player.

A Pattern for Peace

Peace that is based on ignoring truth is dangerous. If peace is to serve as the umpire in our hearts, we must focus on God's definitions and demonstrations of reality. We must practice the teaching handed down to us through His chosen instruments. The apostle Paul gives us the pattern for genuine peace:

> Rejoice in the Lord always. I will say it again: Rejoice! Let your gentleness be evident to all. The Lord is near. Do not be anxious about anything, but in everything, by prayer and petition, with thanksgiving, present your requests to God. And the peace of God, which transcends all understanding, will guard your hearts and your minds in Christ Jesus.
>
> Finally, brothers, whatever is true, whatever is noble, whatever is right, whatever is pure, whatever is lovely, whatever is

admirable—if anything is excellent or praiseworthy—think about such things. Whatever you have learned or received or heard from me, or seen in me—put it into practice. And the God of peace will be with you.[10]

The first issue in living in God's peace is to rejoice in the Lord always (v. 4). Rejoicing entails seeing life from the perspective of Jesus' sovereignty. Since He is king and in complete charge of our lives and all circumstances, we can always rejoice. He has our best interests at heart in spite of what we may see around us to the contrary.

The second instruction for those who want to live in peace involves gentleness (v. 5). It is not our task to condemn all the wrong we see around us. We must certainly discern, but must never make ourselves the judges. It's a great relief to resign from the bench. We don't have to see people who are different as wrong. We can appreciate that many of the differences between other people and ourselves are really complementary. We can bless the distinctions and work with them.

Another key ingredient of a peaceful life is replacing worry with prayer (v. 6). Anyone who makes room for worry has no claim to God's peace. We make room for worry when we justify it, rationalizing that it is our way of being responsible. Instead, this Scripture instructs us to tell God in thankful prayer exactly what concerns us and what we need. If we aren't praying this way, we can't count on the umpire of peace to help us much. But if we do, God's incomprehensible peace will guard our hearts and minds.

The last thing we learn about peaceful living in this passage has to do with our mindset (v. 8). What we fix our thoughts upon determines the measure of our peace. We have control over the direction of our thoughts; this verse tells us which things around us are worthy of our attention. And the best place to find such things is in the lives of godly people around us (v. 9a).

Chaos is curable and peace is available. But the only way to have peace is to submit to the rule and order of God. Mystical subjectivism may cause us to discount God's word in pursuit of existential calm. But the truth is that when God's word enters the picture, genuine salvation, deliverance, and peace are on their way.

Many of us have a verse memorized or on our refrigerator doors: "Seek first his kingdom and his righteousness, and all these things will be given to you."[11] One of the things we need added to our lives is peace. And the way to get it is to seek first God's rule, His kingdom, in every part of our lives. Jesus came to give us the liberty of His peace. And in order to give it to us, He established an order, the kingdom of God, which causes the perpetual increase of peace. His Holy Spirit lives in us to interpret and accomplish that kingdom through our lives. The Body of Christ, the church, helps us to discern what God is saying to us about His kingdom. Our brothers and sisters encourage and instruct us in the ways of God as we learn them together.

When we take advantage of all these resources, we can exhibit self-government. And from that foundation we can build orderly peace in our families, our churches, and our communities. In gradually increasing measure, the prayer that God's will be done on earth as it is in heaven will be answered.

Father, I thank you that You have not left us clueless about peace. There's something inside of us that wants your peace. We would like to have a serenity in our souls that lets us enjoy life and glorify You. We would like to have serenity in our family and in our church and in our government. So Lord, show us how to submit to your sovereignty. Your order. Your reality. Your government. And thank you that You've already given us the Holy Spirit who gives us the capacity to live Jesus' life. We pray in His name. Amen.

LIVING
IN BLESSING

any books on prayer include a chapter or section on breaking curses as a form of prayer. I am fully committed to breaking curses, and though the break may begin with the spoken prayer, the ultimate demise of the curse is the emergence of the blessing. Curses are displaced by blessings. Our prayer focus is toward receiving and transferring the blessing that is ours because of our relationship to Jesus the Lord.

Curses of many kinds plague our modern and technologically advanced world. The stain of racial prejudice still taints the fabric of our public life. What began as a sense of superiority among the majority has elicited a response of heightened racial identity among minority groups. Sexual injustice persists; cruel male chauvinism has given rise to forms of radical feminism. Economic upheaval threatens us even when we enjoy an extended boom in markets. But it is all built on the shifting sands of consumerism and ethical rootlessness. Our families bear the curse of generations of dishonored parents and neglected children.

More than ever, we need to know how to appropriate God's blessings. Our ignorance and disobedience of God's ways has put us in a desperate situation. God gave us laws and precepts to show us how He designed His world to function. He intended us to abide by them and discover destiny and fulfillment. But we have made our own way, and the curses we face are our just inheritance. God still wants to bless rather than curse. And we do well to find out how He wants to do it.

At that time Jesus said,

"I praise you, Father, Lord of heaven and earth, because you have hidden these things from the wise and learned, and revealed them to little children. Yes, Father, for this was your good pleasure.

"All things have been committed to me by my Father. No one knows the Son except the Father, and no one knows the Father except the Son and those to whom the Son chooses to reveal him."[1]

In this exclamation of praise to God the father, Jesus gave us an important clue to the way He wants to bless us today. God wants to bless the world through people who have received and responded to His revelation.

Deliverance by Displacement

One approach to dealing with the obvious curses in our society has been for Christians to become aggressive about breaking them. I've participated in meetings where believers confessed corporate sins, repenting of our own and those of our ancestors. We broke deception and declared the curses null and void. We demanded that the devil cease his work and appealed to God to break the curses Himself. I think all of these things are appropriate. *But genuine deliverance comes through the displacement of curses with blessings.* Since curses are linked to disobedience, at some point blessing begins with obedience.

When Jesus came on the scene, He preached, "The kingdom of God is here." His announcement of His kingdom initiated the demise of the other one. He proclaimed the reign of light over darkness. His ministry brought love to replace hatred and peace to supplant hostility. In His plan, government trumped disorder. Jesus proclaimed and demonstrated a kingdom that is the ultimate expression of displacement.

A focus on getting rid of curses will never release God's people into His blessings. By fixing attention on the negative we miss the whole point of the positive. That kind of approach easily slips into being motivated by the very darkness it seeks to oppose. If our motivation is to live in comfort and tranquillity, with no opposition, we practice the very thing we seek to eliminate. But Jesus invites us to join Him in a strategy of displacement.

I have seen people marvelously and dramatically set free from demonic oppression. And I believe we have the authority of Jesus' name to minister in that way. But if the Holy Spirit and His fruit do not replace the expelled spirit, we haven't helped much. That evil spirit will stand in the corner laughing at us until we leave. Then he'll go to work in the same person with seven of his buddies with him. Getting rid of the negative is only the beginning of the life of blessing we are called to live. God's kingdom conquers by displacing evil with good.

The obvious question, then, is this: How can we experience blessing in our lives instead of curses? We understandably desire God's blessing, not only for ourselves but also for our families, our businesses, our communities, and our nation. The answer is found in the nature of true religion, and *without the revelation of Jesus we will inevitably miss the essence of true religion.* We can too easily find a way to pursue blessing that bypasses listening carefully to Jesus. Only He can reveal the Father to us, and only the Father can reveal the Son to us. So left to ourselves, no matter how religious we are, we will miss the heart of genuine religion.

A passage in the book of James states the practical implications of the religion clearly:

> If anyone considers himself religious and yet does not keep a tight rein on his tongue, he deceives himself and his religion is worthless. Religion that God our Father accepts as pure and faultless is this: to look after orphans and widows in their distress and to keep oneself from being polluted by the world.[2]

This God-inspired description of religion contradicts a lot of current teaching. In our popular systems we get God's blessing by confessing the right truths, developing the right disciplines, or having the right experiences. But none of our ways get to the matters James wants us to high-light: controlling our tongues, taking care of the neediest in society, and keeping ourselves from being polluted by the world.

Manipulation

The great danger is that *in the absence of a true revelation of God we try to manipulate Him.* At the heart of every attempt to manipulate God is the same thought: If I will do a certain thing I can get God to bless me. In Isaiah 58 the prophet addresses this mindset. And we need to examine our hearts in the light of this chapter.

> "Shout it aloud, do not hold back. Raise your voice like a trum-pet. Declare to my people their rebellion and to the house of Jacob their sins. For day after day they seek me out; they seem eager to know my ways, as if they were a nation that does what is right and has not forsaken the commands of its God. They ask me for just decisions and seem eager for God to come near them. 'Why have we fasted,' they say, 'and you have not seen it? Why have we humbled ourselves, and you have not noticed?'
>
> "Yet on the day of your fasting, you do as you please and exploit all your workers. Your fasting ends in quarreling and strife, and in striking each other with wicked fists. You cannot fast as you do today and expect your voice to be heard on high. Is this the kind of fast I have chosen, only a day for a man to humble himself? Is it only for bowing one's head like a reed and

for lying on sackcloth and ashes? Is that what you call a fast, a day acceptable to the LORD?

"Is not this the kind of fasting I have chosen: to loose the chains of injustice and untie the cords of the yoke, to set the oppressed free and break every yoke? Is it not to share your food with the hungry and to provide the poor wanderer with shelter—when you see the naked, to clothe him, and not to turn away from your own flesh and blood? Then your light will break forth like the dawn, and your healing will quickly appear; then your righteousness will go before you, and the glory of the LORD will be your rear guard. Then you will call, and the LORD will answer; you will cry for help, and he will say: Here am I.

"If you do away with the yoke of oppression, with the pointing finger and malicious talk, and if you spend yourselves in behalf of the hungry and satisfy the needs of the oppressed, then your light will rise in the darkness, and your night will become like the noonday. The LORD will guide you always; he will satisfy your needs in a sun-scorched land and will strengthen your frame. You will be like a well-watered garden, like a spring whose waters never fail. Your people will rebuild the ancient ruins and will raise up the age-old foundations; you will be called Repairer of Broken Walls, Restorer of Streets with Dwellings.

"If you keep your feet from breaking the Sabbath and from doing as you please on my holy day, if you call the Sabbath a delight and the LORD's holy day honorable, and if you honor it by not going your own way and not doing as you please or speaking idle words, then you will find your joy in the LORD and I will cause you to ride on the heights of the land and to feast on the inheritance of your father Jacob." The mouth of the LORD has spoken.[3]

Our sinful and independent nature causes us to seek a key, some secret knowledge or act, which unlocks God's blessings for us. We try to use that secret to obligate God in some way to bless us. For Isaiah's audience that secret was fasting and prayer. To all appearances they did everything right. They wore sackcloth and put ashes on their heads. They abstained from food. They prayed and asked God for His word. But the problem was that He didn't answer.

The hardest people I ever deal with are those disillusioned with God for not doing what they expected him to do. They once believed and served God with zeal, but they are on the sidelines today. They may have been involved with some previous movement God blessed for a season. I've met some very wounded people who were involved some years back in a popular movement. They understood God in a certain way, and when God didn't act according to that understanding they got hurt, frustrated, and burned out. The pain and disillusionment they experienced makes them unwilling to commit to anything ever again. Throughout history, other movements have produced the same results in people who were involved.

No one who reads the Bible can doubt the power of prayer and fasting. Praise and thanksgiving are vital habits for a Christian to develop. Confession of sin and declaration of truth are important. But when we use anything to try to obligate God to bless us, we abuse it.

At one time in my life I found myself using contentment to try to manipulate God. I read in the Scriptures that God blesses the heart that rests in Him. So I concentrated on being content with what I had. Before I knew it, I found myself looking to see when God was going to reward my contentment by giving me some new blessing.

I have told many single adults to learn to be content in their unmarried state. I still believe that marriage can easily become an idol for anyone needing companionship. And God is more likely to give a good partner to a Christian who is content to live without a partner. But I saw some singles use contentment as a basis for silently demanding that God give them mates. Contentment became an attempt at manipulation.

Prayer and praise can be misused in the same way. Since one of the Psalms says that God inhabits the praise of His people, many groups approach their worship as a way to get God to come to their meetings. They treat praise as if it were a way to wake God from His sleep and persuade Him to do something He doesn't want to do. They behave as if they don't believe God wants to draw near to them, as if He's waiting for us to press the "call" button.

That sounds too much like the way the prophets of Baal acted on Mount Carmel.[4] Elijah challenged them to call upon their gods to send fire on an altar, after which he would call on his God. Those prophets pushed every button they knew to push. They begged and cajoled; they cut their wrists and bled. They sat, stood, knelt, and lay in every posture available to the human body. All the time they tried to manipulate their god, Elijah mocked them. And Christians who forget who God is can behave the same way and call it "praise and worship."

The deception that God can be manipulated always leads to disillusionment. Isaiah's audience had it. They complained that they'd done all they were supposed to do, but God hadn't done His part. God corrected them, telling them they completely misunderstood the kind of fast He wanted from them. He wanted His people to live a lifestyle that set other people free from their bondage and relieved their pain. He wasn't impressed with their zealous religion. He wanted hungry people fed, naked people clothed, and bound people freed.

Some Christians shrink back from this because it smacks of the old Social Gospel that was preached in the early twentieth century. But that teaching substituted kindness to the needy for a relationship with the living God. We are going after a life that begins with a revelation of God that produces a relationship with Him. From that relationship flows all ministry. It is the only way to break the cycle of manipulation, disillusionment, and inevitable inconsistency.

Inconsistency

When what we are doing in our religious life has no connection to our daily life, inconsistency follows. God called His people down for fasting at the same time they abused workers and took advantage of others in business dealings.[5] Any religious activity that doesn't affect the way we approach the marketplace, the boardroom, and the living room is phony and useless.

Hypocrisy creates internal dissonance that makes a person feel disqualified from engaging the things of God. Church rolls contain the names of thousands of people who don't practice their faith, many not even on Sundays. Most of them dropped out because of their sense of shame over being so inconsistent at practicing what they professed to believe. They disqualified themselves from the race.

Many of the people I'm referring to continue to show respect for God and the church. They may contribute to the offering occasionally. But they are not fully engaged. They contribute little or nothing of the gifts God gave them for the church. As a result they are not fulfilled; they become apathetic or even cynical about the kingdom of God. They misrepresent God because others see their dour countenances and joyless faith and think they see a Christian. No one wants to be around them in case whatever they have is contagious. The inconsistency came out of disillusionment, and the disillusionment arose from attempts to manipulate God.

Recently I was able to spend a couple of days on a ranch in Texas hunting turkey. I didn't get a turkey the whole trip. But it was spring and the bluebonnets were in bloom, filling the air with their fragrance. The birds were singing all around me. All the while I sat under a tree in the middle of the afternoon wearing camouflage from head to toe. I tried to get a gobbler to come up to me by yelping like a turkey hen. For one moment I had a glimpse of the silly reality of the whole scene and started laughing out loud. I was a middle-aged man trying to sound like an attractive lady turkey so a male would let me shoot him. And there was no sign of anything or anyone nearby to hear what I was doing.

The lack of active hunting did give me a great opportunity to think and pray. As I prayed, I battled my own thoughts. I kept hearing myself say, *Why are you asking God about that again? You know God's not likely to give you that. You're too immature to handle it. The last time God gave you something like that you misused it. You're really an embarrassment.* The accusations went on like that.

In the middle of trying to pray through all that, I thought I heard God ask me a question. Now I've learned that when God asks me a question, it's not because He lacks information. He's trying to make a point. So when God asked me, "Why do I bless a person?" I knew enough not to try to answer. Instead, I asked Him, "What do You want to say about that?" And His reply blessed me. He said, "I want to remind you that I bless people not because of anything they do or don't do. I bless because I'm good."

Blessing from Goodness

Though it's a simple truth, we find it hard to walk in its light. The deception runs deep that God blesses because of our goodness instead of His own. But if that were true, none of us would even know God, since none of us was obedient or good to begin with. Paul speaks for all of us:

I thank Christ Jesus our Lord, who has given me strength, that he considered me faithful, appointing me to his service. Even though I was once a blasphemer and a persecutor and a violent man, I was shown mercy because I acted in ignorance and unbelief. The grace of our Lord was poured out on me abundantly, along with the faith and love that are in Christ Jesus. Here is a trustworthy saying that deserves full acceptance: Christ Jesus came into the world to save sinners—of whom I am the worst.[6]

Paul claimed to be the worst blasphemer, the most aggressive persecutor and the most ignorant sinner of all. But in that condition God's mercy came after him and captured him. The same is true of every person God saves. And God's nature doesn't change after He captures us.

When we were lost, God's blessings came out of His goodness and found us. Now that we're His, He doesn't say, "I'm going to change and bless you only when and if you're good." Christ didn't come to save the good and the obedient. He came for those who are lost, confused, deceived, and oppressed. Even those who chose the wrong path can be saved by an encounter with the goodness of Jesus. Had God not expressed His mercy toward us before we sought Him, none of us would know Him.

Some believers are confused by the places in Scripture that indicate, "If you do these things, I will bless you." These are God's invitations for us to discover for ourselves the rhythms of grace He has built into His world. Because God is good He offers blessings. And in those blessings we encounter Him. We don't work a formula or discover a secret, but we encounter Him. His mercy gives us the opportunity to know Him by becoming one with Him. And His nature of goodness begins to supplant the evil in our own hearts so that we give to others out of it. The issue is knowing the One who blesses.

This is not to suggest that there isn't cause and effect built into God's kingdom. There are obviously consequences to our choices. The conflicts resulting from bad choices are designed to redirect our attention to a better way. The issue is the familiar misconception that we only get what we deserve. The good news is that we get what Jesus deserves.

Goodness is not innate with us, but arises from our union—our intimate relationship—with God by the Holy Spirit. That's why Jesus said we are to do good works that will move others to glorify our heavenly Father. They shouldn't be stirred to glorify our strategies or formulas. When they see us being blessed and ask our secret, our answer can't be our prayer life or our praise or our contentment. If we answer that way, people end up glorifying us or the system to which we've attributed our success.

Blessings to Others

If we ever get it right, we will find ourselves acting out of God's nature. We'll offer blessings to those who aren't good, the disqualified and the sinner. Then people will have reason to glorify God for more than our humanitarian compassion. God's people don't feed the poor in order to have a good reputation or clothe the naked in order to be elected to office. Neither do they take care of the needy because they want to build a big church.

Only God and those who know Him would help people who don't deserve help. God makes sun to shine and rain to fall on both the righteous and the wicked. And Jesus told us to treat our enemies no differently than our friends. As we encounter God in His goodness to us, we begin to partake of His very nature of goodness. Then we exhibit that nature in a way that causes onlookers to glorify Him.

People with God's goodness in them want to bless those who need it most and demand it least. They want to care for the widow and orphan and those who are victims of injustice. They want to deal with oppression, both natural and spiritual. For instance, they want to see women who have been abused made whole again as much as they want to see the relationships between men and women set right. They want to see people who are hungry and naked overcome their poverty and the sense of inferiority it breeds. Such a person will pray for the needy with clothes on one arm and a sack of groceries in the other.

Ministry to the poor begins with the understanding that poverty is a symptom. No amount of money spent or homes built or clothing distributed will address the root of the problem. A spirit of poverty has to be supplanted by a habit of stewardship. Only then will blessing permanently displace curse in the lives of the needy.

God is looking for a religion that comes from the depths of a person who knows Him personally in Jesus Christ. Such deep knowledge begins an outward flow of kindness motivated by delight in God. That quality of kindness is so different that the world wants to know the God who produces it.

An Increase in Blessing

The kind of life I've been describing has an inherent complication with it. When we begin to tap into God's goodness, His blessing increases on our lives. It may come in the form of finances or wisdom or other resources, but the blessing begins to flow through our lives. To an outsider it looks like prosperity, but we understand that we are only conduits of God's goodness. We have one hand reaching out to God in neediness and another reaching out to other needy people. So at any given moment, a snapshot of our lives may reveal a large quantity of available resources. In fact, this is the life God designed us to live.

Jesus demonstrated just this kind of life here on earth. He simply said and did what He heard and saw the Father doing. He gave away what the Father gave Him, and He judged only after He knew the Father's discernment. He didn't bless toward goodness, but out of goodness. And His goodness flowed toward the needy rather than the deserving. He was a clear channel God used to bless others.

Isaiah 58 contains some wonderful promises for those who live this way:

Their prayers will be answered (v. 9).

Their depression and self-centeredness will end (v. 10).

Divine guidance will increase (v. 11).

Foundations and breaches will be restored (v. 12).

Promises like these excite us and motivate us. But the only way to live in such a blessing is to become a conduit, rather than a container. In practical terms, that means we must focus on God enough to discover for ourselves that He is different than we've been led to believe. He isn't the push-button deity that human religion has devised. The key to knowing Him is not to discover some arcane secret but to draw on His great goodness with our deep neediness.

He is good and what He does is good. An encounter with God will cause us to redefine our understanding of goodness. A renewed focus on God's goodness will produce an increase of gratefulness. Even what seemed bad will start to look like an expression of the mercy and kindness of God.

Actually Changed

Another added blessing to our lives is the recognition of knowing God has imparted His goodness within us. There's something inside us that delights to bless the disqualified and detests injustice and oppression, nakedness and poverty. Some of us have complained about the government's interference in these areas. But it's time for Christians to get the planks out of our own eyes on this issue. When we do, we'll see beyond ourselves to the people near us who need help and the circumstances around us that need change.

We can ask God to open our eyes to the wrong around us. Then we can stop griping about it and start doing something redemptive. For instance, we have complained for years that actors and athletes are wealthy while schoolteachers barely survive. And the situation is magnified in most Christian schools. I long for the day that Christian education will be valued enough for us to pay teachers in Christian schools more than the public schools. When are we going to get tired of being the tail and not the head?[7]

If we really believed in godly education, we might deal with this inequity more productively. Any Christian can find a believing teacher who needs financial help. Many of us will pay one hundred dollars to take our families to a professional ball game or popular concert, but will never give that much to a teacher. So we are part of the problem we decry.

Isaiah 58 has some amazing, practical implications for any of us who have gotten "too religious" to be helpful. If we truly know God, there is within us an impulse to be a blessing. James agrees when, in chapter 2 of his epistle, he says we should not give preference to the well heeled who show up at our church meetings. Instead we should recognize the grace God shows to the needy.

God has always blessed us when we didn't deserve it. Since we are in that flow of mercy, we too must give what we have to those who don't deserve or demand it. The issue will never be the good we do, but the Good One we know. The blessings God promises us are only the by-product, never the purpose, for our mercy toward others. We can begin eliminating the curse on our land when we understand and appropriate the truth about God's goodness.

This is the very reason Jesus came to show us the Father. Everything else we hear and see is a form of religious cover-up. James reminds us that if our religion doesn't cause us to be involved with the neediest among us, it is fundamentally faulty. True religion begins with a relationship with a God who blesses us—and others through us—because He is good.

As we embrace this life of true religion, we will certainly displace the darkness left behind by false religion. The kingdom will come everywhere true religion is practiced.

Father, I pray that You'll help us to see this simple but powerful revelation. We can't see it if You don't open our eyes to see it. And so we ask for that grace today. Thank you for blessing us because of your goodness. Thank you for the privilege to bless because You're good in us and we can be good in You. In Jesus' name, Amen.

PRAYING
IN THE SPIRIT

In the same way, the Spirit helps us in our weakness.
We do not know what we ought to pray for, but the Spirit himself
intercedes for us with groans that words cannot express.
And he who searches our hearts knows the mind of the Spirit, because
the Spirit intercedes for the saints in accordance with God's will.

ROMANS 8:26–27

I had been away from the family for several days on a ministry trip. Each night I looked forward to the phone call home to find out how my wife, son, and daughter were doing. These phone calls usually were characterized by much joy and the thrill of getting to talk to each of the kids on the phone, hearing the details of their day. After a tiring day of work, I always looked forward to the refreshment that came from those calls to home.

It was Wednesday night; I would be going home early Thursday morning. This phone call was about to change my life. When my wife, Betsy, picked up the phone I could tell something was wrong. She began to relate to me the severe pain she was having in her arm. It was so severe she couldn't sleep. She had bright red stripes up and down her arm.

From her training as a nurse, Betsy knew something was severely wrong. Meekly she said, "It only started this morning. Now it's all over my whole arm and even my shoulder. I think it might be staph infection."

Then she related how earlier that day she'd taken Karis by the doctor to have a checkup. The doctor reported he thought she might be a candidate for juvenile diabetes. But that wasn't all. Our son David had swallowed a tack earlier in the day and had already been taken to the emergency room.

I wanted to gather all of my family into my arms, but I was a thousand miles away. It was late at night—there was no way I could get there until the next day. All I could do was pray.

That night as I knelt beside a bed in a dreary motel room, I found that my burden was greater than my ability to express. All I could do was groan. Every once in a while I could make out some intelligible words like "Oh, God!" and "Mercy." But putting together an intelligible, rational prayer was beyond my ability. I really don't know how long this prayer session went on—it seemed like an eternity—but finally there was an answer that floated to my consciousness: "Your wife will be fine in a few days. Your daughter's illness is an opportunity for you and your wife to learn faith. Your son is in no danger."

I can't explain how I knew that those words were from my heavenly Father. I can only testify that I knew. I also knew that I had experienced an encounter with God in prayer that was different from anything I'd had before. God had come to me and helped me pray a prayer that He was now answering. I was learning what I've been trying to say throughout this whole book: God is so interested in our prayer life, He not only starts our prayer life and ends it, He also comes to us and helps us pray.

> We do not know what we ought to pray for, but the Spirit himself intercedes for us with groans that words cannot express.[1]

Weakness No Obstacle

The first thing we learn about Holy Spirit–assisted prayer is that our weaknesses don't disqualify us from participating in eternal purposes. Prayer is our part; it is our privilege and responsibility, but we can't fulfill that responsibility apart from God's intervening and helping us. It is His mercy from first to last.

The eighth chapter of Romans is one of the most beautiful passages of Scripture in all the Bible, for it describes the life given to us through faith in Jesus Christ. This life was imparted to us by the presence of the Holy Spirit, who has united with our spirit.[2]

LIFE TO OUR BODIES

First, we're told that the Holy Spirit came into us to give life to our mortal bodies. Those bodies that were dead because of sin are granted the ability to have the very life of Jesus in them. We're not just the chemical components of a fleshly body; actually we're clay vessels inhabited by the very presence of God.[3]

AN INTIMATE RELATIONSHIP

Second, the Holy Spirit came into us to make our relationship with God an intimate one.

> For you did not receive a spirit that makes you a slave again to fear, but you received the Spirit of sonship. And by him we cry, "Abba, Father."[4]

It is the Holy Spirit's revelation to our inner man that God is no longer just the creator of the universe and the judge of all mankind, but He is the heavenly Father to those who come to Him by faith in Christ Jesus. This is no longer just a cognitive knowledge, but now a real experience for those who enjoy the ministry of the Holy Spirit in their hearts.

CHILDREN OF GOD

Third, the Holy Spirit witnesses to our spirit that we are the children of God.

> The Spirit himself testifies with our spirit that we are God's children.[5]

We are no longer left to simple, rational propositions to believe that we are the children of God. We can know from an inner knowing that we are His children and are safe in His hands. Apart from the ministry of the Holy Spirit, this knowledge is left to our memory or rational deduction.

HELP IN OUR WEAKNESS

Fourth, the Holy Spirit helps us in our weakness.

In the same way, the Spirit helps us in our weakness.[6]

This phrase comes in the context of a passage where Paul discussed the groaning of creation as it awaits its final redemption. He described the conflict that we have as human beings who are part of a fallen creation, yet are indwelt by eternal life. While creation groans, waiting for the children of God to be revealed and for the culmination of the kingdom of God, we as believers experience something of the limitation of human beings. Yet this conflict of our limitations does not prohibit us from participating in God's eternal plan for us.

God created us to rule on the earth with Him through our prayers. It is such an incredible thought that God allows us, feeble human beings, to participate in His eternal purposes, and that He comes to assist us in knowing how to pray.

Times of Groaning

All who have taken prayer seriously have experienced those times of groaning. We know we should pray, we even want to pray, but we don't know how to pray. We may have concerns for our own family, for instance. We don't know whether to pray that our children never have trouble or to pray that they'll have trouble so they'll discover the grace of God. Regarding our financial condition, do we pray for more resources or do we pray that God will give us a contentment with the things we already have? As we pray for our nation, do we pray for prosperity or do we pray that the nation experience more crises, so that we'll repent and return to the God who is the source of all our blessing? These and a thousand other issues can become a point of consternation for us when we have taken seriously the mandate from our Creator to manage this earth through prayer.

The positively good news of this passage is that, through my groans and the assistance of the Holy Spirit, I can pray beyond my understanding. If my prayers are answered based on my intelligence, or even my purist motives, I can be assured that many, if not most, prayers would go unanswered. This passage gives me hope that, when I've come to the end of myself and don't even know how to express my prayer, the Holy Spirit will come to my aid and assist me by praying both for me and through me.

Maybe we should point out that the experience of groaning can be offensive. None of us likes to be in a position where we are out of control, but when the burden is so deep that we can't express it fully, we are in a place beyond our understanding. I don't know about you, but when I pray I've found that my head fights to get ahead of my heart. And all the while God seeks to build up my inner man so that I am ruled more by my spirit than just my thoughts.

For who among men knows the thoughts of a man except the man's spirit within him? In the same way no one knows the thoughts of God except the Spirit of God. We have not received the spirit of the world but the Spirit who is from God, that we may understand what God has freely given us.[7]

For this reason I kneel before the Father, from whom his whole family in heaven and on earth derives its name. I pray that out of his glorious riches he may strengthen you with power through his Spirit in your inner being.[8]

Groaning is not a very sophisticated way to pray. It doesn't give much solace to our pride and independent self-esteem. Many times we seek to avoid situations that make us desperate, but it's been accurately said, "It is only when the desperation factor exceeds our embarrassment factor that we are open to a new work from God."

The Spiritual Gifts

My theological training taught me to base all of my theology on Scripture. One of my favorite professors in seminary once said, "Interpret the Scripture first and develop your theology second. If you do it in reverse order, you'll never know what God says." Because I believe that's true, it was my conclusion that all the spiritual gifts God gave to the early church are still available today.

In my experience, however, I honestly didn't see the need for some spiritual gifts, especially those that were causing controversy in the early

1970s when I was pastor of a small church. I had carefully examined the Scriptures regarding spiritual gifts, hoping that I could find evidence that at least some of the gifts had passed away. I could easily see the need for gifts such as teaching and wisdom. But other gifts, like prophecy and tongues, seemed to be causing more controversy and separation than blessing. Staying true to my commitment to the Scriptures, I concluded that all the gifts were available. But I can tell you honestly that I didn't seek all of them.

However, as my heart became hungrier to see God move in His church and in the world, I began praying for revival. I even traveled around the country, helping to promote conferences about the nature of revival and awakening. It was at one of those conferences that God obviously thought we were serious, and He came in a measure of revival. As a result, there were all kinds of manifestations of need and God's provision. Sick people started getting well. Demonized people were delivered. People addicted to drugs stopped taking them in miraculous fashion. Unbelievers were converted, and believers became enthusiastic and excited by the conscious presence of God.

I found myself spending hours a day dealing with pastors and their people over issues like demons and severe diseases. I realized that these people needed neither a theological treatise on specific doctrines nor the counseling that I'd learned from my Christian psychology. What they needed was an encounter with the power of God in the person of the Holy Spirit.

To sum it up, when continually faced with people whose bodies are racked by demonization or are being destroyed by cancer, you become open to gifts that previously didn't seem necessary. This was my case. I found myself praying like this:

> Father, I want all the gifts that You have written in all the lists in your Bible, and if those are just representative, I want all the ones that You could have written down had You chosen to do so.

Finally, the passage where Paul said "eagerly desire spiritual gifts"[9] had meaning for me. I was now able to obey that Scripture with my whole heart.

Praying in Tongues

I'm sure the question arises, "Does this passage in Romans, chapter 8, speak of praying in tongues?" There has been disagreement among scholars about this. It seems to me that this passage would include the ability to pray in tongues, but it doesn't describe that experience exclusively. We can pray in the Spirit whether we are using the gift of tongues or not. Just like we live in the Spirit and walk in the Spirit, we can pray in the Spirit, which essentially means to pray with a consciousness that the Holy Spirit is motivating our prayer, guiding our prayer, and answering our prayer. It is an attitude of total dependence upon God to align our will with His will, which helps us express the burdens of our heart and receive the blessings that He intended.

It's unfortunate that praying in tongues has become controversial in the body of Christ and has caused many to retreat from the privilege of praying in the Spirit. We don't have to be afraid of anything that God gives. It is for His glory and our good. The ability to pray in tongues is a gift from God that allows us to communicate with God spirit-to-Spirit, without the full use of understanding.

> For anyone who speaks in a tongue does not speak to men but to God. Indeed, no one understands him; he utters mysteries with his spirit.[10]

Since it's a gift, it's something we must receive when we desire it, ask for it, and believe it. Obviously, if we don't want it, then God doesn't force that gift upon us. The benefit of the gift is that it edifies the believer.

> He who speaks in a tongue edifies himself, but he who prophesies edifies the church.[11]

Some have concluded that it is wrong to want to edify self. I don't believe Paul, here, was referring to the egocentric self, but rather he was talking about one's whole being. It isn't wrong to want to be edified—that is, to be energized and built up in the spirit. We study the Scriptures for that purpose. We pray and meditate for that purpose. We fast and practice solitude and silence for that purpose. We listen to tapes and attend conferences, all so our spirit can be edified.

Desire for edification is not self-centered. It is what we do as a result of our edification that determines whether or not our motive is pure. If we try to use any gift that we have from God as a trophy to prove our spirituality, then we've moved from servanthood to idolatry. If we use it as a toy to play with, we are revealing our immaturity. If we use it as a tool that God has given to us to subdue the earth in partnership with Him, then we have properly found the use of His gift.

As we said earlier, this passage in Romans probably isn't referring directly to the gift of tongues when it speaks of the Holy Spirit coming and helping us in our weaknesses. The implication here is not that He prays in our stead, but that He helps us to pray. He takes what is inexpressible in our mind and turns it into a viable prayer. We mustn't lose the glory of this blessing in all the questions we may have about how it works. The bottom line is that God has graced us with the person of the Holy Spirit to give us life, to guide us in life, and even to help us pray when the prayers we need go beyond our human limitations. We can pray beyond our understanding by relying on the Holy Spirit.

Fruits of Spirit-Assisted Prayer

Spirit-assisted prayer, in its end, is fruitful. First of all, the Holy Spirit always prays according to the will of God since He is God himself. The Holy Spirit prays according to the sovereign purposes of God. If we want to know what He's praying, we can again become acquainted with those sovereign purposes. He is able to take the mystery of the burdens of our hearts, mix it with the sovereign purposes of God, and come out with a prayer that pleases the Father and gets an answer.

This type of prayer also releases burdens. Many people go through life totally burdened down, not understanding that many of those burdens are God's call for their involvement in His eternal purposes. Many spend their whole life trying to get out from under the burden without praying. The burden is there as our invitation to come to God and be a part of the divine enterprise. When we yield to Holy Spirit–assisted praying, we find burdens lifted from us that could never be taken away by counseling, drugs, or religious activity. They are there to bring us into that total dependence upon our Father, who desires so desperately to bless us with His life.

Another fruit of Holy Spirit–assisted praying is that it activates our faith. It requires faith to pray with a groan. We have to believe in the promises of God, that He is actually doing something in us in order for us to pray like this. In this type of praying, not only can we not figure out how God is going to answer it, we can't figure out how to ask it. This kind of praying activates our faith, and faith pleases God.

Well, this kind of takes away all of our excuses, doesn't it? We can no longer say, "I don't pray because I don't know how." God, in essence, says, "I'll come and pray with you and for you." We also can't say, "Well, I'm too burdened to pray." The burden is the call to pray. We can't say, "I'm afraid to pray. I'm afraid I'll pray with the wrong motives," for God has said that He'll help us pray according to His will. With no excuses left, our only recourse is to accept our role as God has defined it—to pray, "Thy kingdom come, thy will be done on earth as it is in heaven."

Father, thank you for being so intent on our participation with You in accomplishing eternal purposes. Thank you for the ministry of the Holy Spirit, who comes to our aid to help us pray beyond our capabilities. Thank you for the burdens that call us to prayer. And finally, thank you for answering the prayer You started in our hearts. Amen.

CHAPTER ELEVEN

PRAYING FOR OTHERS

As a young pastor, I felt most uncomfortable making the initial visit to a family member after an unexpected tragedy. Classes in pastoral counseling in seminary had assured me that words were not the issue in those situations, but as a preacher, words were my most effective tools. Without them, I felt useless.

One day I said to a grieving widow, whose husband had died suddenly in the prime of life, "I wish I had something to say." She looked at me gratefully through eyes of pain and said, "Just your being here makes all the difference." As I drove home that night, I tried thinking through that dynamic again. Why did my presence matter? I wasn't saying anything that made a difference. I was just taking up space—or was I?

My thoughts drifted to Jesus, the ultimate intercessor. Is it what He says in the presence of the throne of heaven that makes the difference on earth for me, or just the fact that He is there? He intercedes because of who He is, not because of what He does. He is the Son of Man who represents us. He is the Son of God who represents God. He has already paid the eternal price for all of my disqualifying sins. Just His being there makes possible my constant communion and conscious communication with God. Could it be that my privileged assignment as an intercessor is not based upon just what I say, but the presence of who I am?

Being and Doing

There has always been a tension between our being and our doing. The pendulum seems to swing from one emphasis to the other. Some are so interested in *being* that they never seem to get around to *doing* anything worthwhile. Others are so into the activist mode that they are unable to enjoy the benefit of *being* in Christ.

As we discussed earlier, prayer in any form is as much a matter of who we are as what we say. If we focus on saying without doing, we become hypocrites. If we focus on doing without being, we run the risk of developing a presumptuous attitude toward our influence. On the "being" side of our intercession, we must appreciate the fact that we've been made ambassadors on this earth, representing another government.

All this is from God, who reconciled us to himself through Christ and gave us the ministry of reconciliation: that God was reconciling the world to himself in Christ, not counting men's sins against them. And he has committed to us the message of reconciliation. We are therefore Christ's ambassadors, as though God were making his appeal through us. We implore you on Christ's behalf: Be reconciled to God.[1]

One of the beautiful pictures of Jesus interceding for His disciples came after He'd performed the miracle of multiplying a few loaves of bread and a couple fish to feed a multitude.[2] He had told His disciples to get into the boat and go to the other side. When they reached about midpoint in the lake, a major storm whipped up and began to threaten their very lives. While they were in the midst of this apparent tragedy, Jesus was on the mountain watching them and praying for them. They didn't know it, but they were secure because they were being held by Someone who, because of who He was, was being heard in what He said.

We too can take great comfort that Jesus, today, is in heaven interceding for us.

> Therefore he is able to save completely those who come to God through him, because he always lives to intercede for them.[3]

I don't get the impression that Jesus is in heaven saying a lot of prayers. It's the fact that He's already there as the once-and-for-all sin offering for our sins that makes possible our constant communication with the Father.

While Jesus is in heaven, interceding for us by who He is and what He says, we've been given the privilege of being His representatives of heaven on earth. We represent Him by being the sons of the kingdom and by praying according to His will, then obeying our instructions. He represents us in heaven. We represent Him on earth. What a great privilege...this thing of intercession.

Intercessory Prayer

In Luke 11 we have a great teaching by Jesus on prayer. First He goes through what we normally call the Lord's Prayer. Then He continues His teaching by telling a story regarding intercessory prayer. The story goes something like this:

A man is asleep at midnight when a knock comes at his door. When he answers the door, he finds a friend who is destitute and hungry. The friend is asking for food. The problem is the host has no food. He says to his friend, "Sit here in my house and I'll be back."

He then goes to his neighbor and knocks on his door. The neighbor doesn't answer because of the lateness of the hour. Finally, because the man won't stop knocking, the neighbor comes to the door to find out what the problem is.

"A friend of mine has stopped on his journey and is hungry, and I have nothing to give him," says the man. "Please give me three loaves of bread."

The neighbor is incensed that he would be disrupted in the middle of his sleep by the neighbor who has come for someone else's need. He answers, "This is very inconvenient. It's going to awaken my whole family. Why don't you come back at a more convenient time?"

The man refuses to give in and insists that his neighbor give him food for his hungry friend. Finally, because he won't quit knocking, the neighbor relents and gives him what he requests. (paraphrase mine)

ANOTHER'S NEED BECOMES OUR OWN

In this story, there are three aspects to intercession. First, we are intercessors when another's need becomes our own. The man is not bothering his neighbor because he himself is hungry, but because someone has come to him and he has assumed their hunger as his own.

This reality is illustrated for us throughout Scripture. God was ready to wipe out the whole nation of Israel because of their rebellious acts while Moses was on the mountain receiving instructions. When God suggested He devastate the whole nation and start over with Moses, Moses was an intercessor. His plea was, essentially, "If you're going to wipe them out, wipe me out too." Moses, though not guilty of the people's sin, was willing to so identify with them that he accepted the responsibility for their sin. In the face of this intercession, God had mercy on the people and continued to guide them on their journey.

And of course, Jesus, the ultimate intercessor, is able to say, "I forgive you," because He was willing to take our sins on His body on the cross. He who knew no sin became sin for us so that we could know His righteousness. We see it also illustrated after Jesus' resurrection in the life of Paul, who prayed for his fellow kinsmen, the Israelites, saying to God that he would himself be willing to be accursed for the sake of his kinsmen.[4]

But there are so many needs in the world and so many needy people— how do we know for whom we're to intercede? In the previous chapter we discussed praying in the Spirit and suggested that one of the ways that the Holy Spirit leads us in prayer is by allowing us to carry the same burdens that are on God's heart at a particular time. I think we can safely say that the presence of a genuine burden is the call to intercession. However, it's the choice to take it to Jesus that is the act of intercession. Too many people feel like they're intercessors simply because they carry heavy burdens. We must remember that we are not the ultimate intercessor. Jesus is. It is our responsibility not to bear the burdens, but to take them to Jesus. His shoulders are broad enough to carry any burden we can bring to Him.

DEPENDING ON RESOURCES BEYOND OURSELVES

The second aspect of intercession revealed in this story is that we are true intercessors when we depend on resources that are beyond ourselves. The man in the story was an intercessor because he fully recognized that he didn't have the wherewithal to grant his friend's request. I think modern Christians sometimes confuse the call to intercede with a call to be a messiah. All of us need to be needed, but sometimes we find a perverted joy in so identifying with others' problems that we become entangled with them. It reminds me of a story in the life of John the Baptist.

John the Baptist had inaugurated his ministry out in the wilderness and was drawing great crowds.[5] The religious leaders of the day sent a committee to find out if he was the Messiah or the prophet who would precede the Messiah. When they interviewed John, he gave them a very clear and precise answer: "I am not the Christ."

Many of us could learn from John and eliminate much of the anxiety in our lives if we could agree that we are not anyone's messiah. We've been sent to earth as ambassadors from the kingdom of God in order to see burdens and take them quickly to Jesus, who is the Messiah. If we find ourselves giving needy people something to do rather than someone to meet, we know that we've moved away from being true intercessors. God isn't trying to establish more codependent relationships among needy people. What He is seeking is to give us the privilege of bearing the burdens of others to the shoulders of Jesus, who can reveal to those in need His glory and set them free from their preoccupation with sin and self.

Oftentimes I find myself optimistic that God can move in the behalf of another whose problem doesn't seem so big. However, when the problem is beyond my ability to see how it can be fixed, I tend to move toward doubt. The truth is, it doesn't take any more of a miracle of God to save a "bad" sinner than it does a "good" person. Although I'm ashamed to admit it, there were people I knew who were so belligerent toward God and His things that I was sure they'd committed the unpardonable sin, or that God had chosen to use them as illustrations to show how bad a person can be in a life without God. To my pleasant but unexpected surprise, I found these men later in life to have become great spiritual leaders in their communities. So much for my great discernment.

THE SOLUTION IS A PRIORITY

The third aspect of intercession seen here is that we can know we're intercessors when getting the solution becomes a priority. Intercession is not just a matter of tossing up some casual requests before God and then for-getting about them. The man in the story was so determined to get an answer, he was willing to risk his neighbor's respect and friendship. He had to have an answer!

Answers to All the Problems

The answers to all the problems in this world are in one of three places. They're in heaven because we haven't asked for or received them. Or the answers are in our hearts because we've asked for them and received them by promise, but they've yet to manifest. Or they're in our hand because we've asked for them and, by our persistent faith, have finally received the manifestation of God's will being done on earth.

So how does it work? Maybe we can learn a lesson from the incident in Mark 11:12–26. One day as Jesus and His disciples were leaving Bethany and going toward Jerusalem, Jesus saw a fig tree. Because He was hungry, He went to look for some figs on the tree. He found it had leaves, but no fruit. He simply spoke to the tree and told it to die. They went on into the city. The next morning as they came back, Peter saw the tree and was astounded that it had withered and dried up so quickly. Jesus, using this as an attention-getter, taught an essential truth about believing prayer:

> "Have faith in God," Jesus answered. "I tell you the truth, if anyone says to this mountain, 'Go, throw yourself into the sea,' and does not doubt in his heart but believes that what he says

will happen, it will be done for him. Therefore I tell you, whatever you ask for in prayer, believe that you have received it, and
it will be yours. And when you stand praying, if you hold anything against anyone, forgive him, so that your Father in heaven
may forgive you your sins." [6]

Purified Desires

There are several key words in these verses that are pregnant with insight.
First of all, Jesus talked about what we *ask* for in prayer—in other words,
what we *desire,* to use a term found in some translations of this passage.
Desire is an important part of our lives. God, contrary to many idealists,
is not interested in eradicating our desires. He is, however, very interested
in purifying them. A person who has no desire has no passion. A person
who has perverted desires is dangerous.

The Intercessor we have in heaven has the same desires as the heavenly Father. Those desires are for His Father to be glorified and for us to
be blessed. God continually works to purify our desires so that we operate on earth in line with His will as much as Jesus operates in heaven in
line with His will. Oftentimes we pray according to our desires, and God
has to work on our desires.

Jesus gave a great analogy of our relationship with Him when He
said, "I am the vine; you are the branches."[7] As we visualize how a vine
and a branch work together, we can see that the vine is the main stem
and the branch shoots off from it. The vine is responsible for the sap and
all the life-giving power. It is the source of life, if you will. The branch is

simply attached to the vine. The good news is that everything that's in the vine can belong to the branch if the branch is living in union with the vine. If some blockage comes between the branch and the vine, even though all of that life in the vine is available, it's never appropriated.

In reality we are the branches, and God wants to share with us everything He has—His knowledge, His wisdom, His power, His possessions, His protection, and yes, His desires.

It's all right to pray our desires. If our desires are impure, God will redirect our praying. We can remember the story of the man who had the demonized son. He'd come up to Jesus' disciples and asked them for help. They were unable to help, so they brought the man to Jesus. His first request was that Jesus deliver his son from the demons. In Jesus' response to him, He indicates that anything is possible to the one who believes. The man then changes his prayer from asking for deliverance for his son to asking Jesus to give him faith. "I do believe; help me overcome my unbelief!"[8]

Pray Boldly

Another phrase that's essential to our understanding of prayer is the almost astounding statement that Jesus made: "Believe that you have received it." These are incredible words. Notice that He did not say, "Believe that you shall receive it," but rather, "Believe that you have received it"[9] (emphasis mine). Once we learn to pray with confidence according to desires that have been purified by God Himself, we are to pray boldly. Now is no time for intimidation. It is certainly no time for false humility. We've been sent as ambassadors of heaven to represent God on the earth. It is our privilege and responsibility to identify the needs, bring them to Jesus, and then to pray boldly for Him to answer.

Does this suggest a boldness inconsistent with the humility of a contrite saint? I think not. A person who will do anything that God asks will have the boldness to ask God anything. I don't believe Abraham was filled with timidity when he was interceding for Sodom. He so identified with the people there that he went boldly to God to ask for His mercy. It's evident from this story that Abraham was willing to do anything God would have asked him to do in relationship to Sodom. When we're willing to be absolute in our obedience to God, He is willing to be absolute in His commitment to releasing heaven in our circumstances. There are occasions when soft meditations and reflections in prayer are not what are called for. It's time for the bold saint to speak to the mountain and tell it to move.

This is no encouragement to be presumptuous, but rather an encouragement to total commitment to the Lord of mercy and to absolute obedience to instructions. We can do nothing greater as intercessors than to pray and obey. It isn't pleasing to God for us to leave answers to prayer in heaven. The answers to our prayers were given before the foundation of the world.

Now we who have believed enter that rest, just as God has said, "So I declared on oath in my anger, 'They shall never enter my rest.'" And yet his work has been finished since the creation of the world.[10]

We are to stay at the door and knock until we get an answer. Some-times the answer is that God moves it from heaven to our heart. That is, in answer to our prayer, He gives the assurance that it's already been answered as far as He is concerned. Then it's our privilege to wait for its manifestation until, one day, we can have it in our hand.

BELIEVE YOU HAVE RECEIVED GOD'S PROMISE

As a freshman in college, I had accepted an invitation to be a counselor at a youth camp in Oklahoma. During that youth camp I encountered God in new and more intimate ways. I was made aware of the reality of the fullness of the Holy Spirit. Before, my life had been characterized by dedication, rededication, and more rededication. I had finally come to understand a little bit of what it means to "rest in the fullness of the Spirit." It was such a joy to discover that His work in me didn't depend upon my striving but upon His promises.

During that camp I accepted the invitation of a pastor to lead a youth crusade in his church. My roommate in college and another friend I'd met in camp went to be the leadership of this crusade. We were fully aware of our incompetence in doing what we'd been assigned to do, so we spent every moment we could praying or reading Scripture.

Much of what we did could be characterized as zealous ignorance, but with a pure heart. Together we studied the book of Acts and noticed that the early church waited for the Holy Spirit until they heard the sound of rushing, mighty wind and saw tongues of fire. We stayed up most of every night, praying for the same manifestations that the early church had seen at Pentecost (one night we were actually arrested by the local police because they found us in the church office at three o'clock in the morning).

Finally, after several nights of praying as hard and as loud as we knew how, it seemed as if God spoke very quietly to us and said, "Are you willing to believe that you already have what I promised you?" It seemed like all the air was filled with the life-giving energy of the presence of God. There was no sound of rushing, mighty wind, no tongues of fire, and yet there was a great peace in my heart. God had answered my prayer. I neither prophesied nor spoke in tongues, but I walked out of that church office assured that I was filled with the same Spirit who had come on the day of Pentecost. I simply believed that I had already received it. It wasn't a matter of my talking myself into it. It was a matter of believing what God had promised.

Since that day I've had many other wonderful experiences in praying for others when God gave me the assurance in my heart that He'd heard my prayer. It was left for me to be obedient in relationship to them. No longer was the burden acute. I was privileged to listen to the direction of the Spirit as he moved the answer from my heart to my hand. Sometimes the answer was days in coming, sometimes months, sometimes years, but I had and still have the confidence of knowing that I stayed at the door and knocked until He answered.

PRAYING FOR
THE LOST

I was pastor of a small Baptist church during seminary days. It was one of the great experiences of my life. I really feel embarrassed by the quality of pastoring that the people had, but I shall forever be grateful to God and those people for the opportunity to learn in such a safe environment.

It was my custom in those days to visit weekly in the homes of those who had never professed Jesus Christ as their savior. One of the people I met in my evangelistic visiting was a young man named Ronnie. Ronnie was very courteous and received me into his home graciously. I asked if I could share the gospel with him, to which he agreed. He listened intently. When I concluded, I asked if he felt any conviction in his heart for his sin and his need for a savior. He thanked me for my presentation, but said that he didn't feel any need to have that kind of relationship with God. He assured me that I was always welcome in his home for further discussion.

Periodically I stopped by Ronnie's house and visited with him, often sharing Scripture related to our need for God and the privilege of trusting Jesus as savior. Ronnie continued to insist that he had no conscious need of a saving relationship with Christ. Of course, Ronnie was placed on my daily prayer list. I prayed for him consistently according to the Scriptures that we will deal with below.

One night, in the wee hours of the morning, I awoke. I decided to go over my prayer list for lost sinners. As I began to pray for Ronnie, I sensed in my spirit that the answer was moving from heaven to my heart. Joy flooded my heart as I lay in bed at three o'clock in the morning. (Can anything give joy at three o'clock in the morning?) God had answered. I was so sure that Ronnie had decided to give his life to Christ, I could hardly wait to get to his house the next day.

During those days I attended classes at seminary, so I was unable to visit Ronnie until late afternoon. Finally I got to his house, knocked on his door, and yelled out through the screen door, "Ronnie, did you trust Christ last night?" He answered back, "No. I don't think so. Would you like to come in?"

I was stunned by his answer. I had so expected him to say, "Yes."

"No," I said, "I've got to be going. I just wanted to check and see. I'll talk with you later."

As I got in my car and drove away, I was a little confused. I thought certainly, in my prayer the night before, God had said, "It is done." As I questioned God while driving, it seemed that I could hear this question floating through my conscience: "Who are you going to believe—Ronnie or Me?" I breathed a prayer of thanksgiving. "Father, thank you for answering my prayer. Now show me how to harvest this fruit."

I continued to befriend Ronnie and stop by his house for friendly fellowship. A few months after this event, I started the ministry I lead today and resigned as pastor of that church, so I didn't see Ronnie after that.

A little over a year later, I was asked by the church to come back as the speaker at a homecoming event. As I stood at the front after speaking, shaking hands with old friends, I saw Ronnie run down the aisle. He grabbed me by both arms and said, "Hey, man! Did you hear what happened?" "No," I said. "What?" "Well, I was out in the backyard with my children, and it was as if scales fell off my eyes. I could see that I was a sinner in need of a savior—just like all those Scriptures you used to read to me—and I trusted Christ in my own backyard." As Ronnie and I embraced at the front of the church, I thanked God profusely for the answer that had finally moved not only from heaven to my heart, but now from my heart to my hand. The fruit had been harvested.

Jesus Deserves His Reward

God loves to save sinners. We can be confident when we pray for sinners to be saved by the grace of God though Jesus Christ. First of all, Jesus deserves the trophy of His work. It is always God's will to glorify His Son. He glorifies His Son by giving Him the rewards of His labor. Because Jesus lived, suffered, died, and was resurrected so that lost sinners could be saved, the Father continues to bless the Son by bringing sinners to salvation. He uses us in that process because we are His representatives on the earth.

The primary motivation for evangelism is not just that lost sinners are going to hell, but that Jesus, the Son of God, deserves the reward of

His labor. Many people excuse their lack of praying for the lost or evangelizing the lost on the grounds that they don't actually love the lost. They assume there are some people who are overwhelmingly in love with rebellious sinners. The issue is not so much a love for the lost as it is a love for the Savior.

Do you remember the story of Jesus confronting Peter after the resurrection?[1] They were sitting around the fire on the beach that morning when Jesus said to Peter, "Do you truly love me more than these?" Peter responded in the affirmative. Jesus' answer was, "Feed my lambs." The second time Jesus asked, "Do you truly love me?" and again, Peter responded affirmatively. Jesus said again, "Take care of my sheep." Even the third time when Jesus asked, "Do you love me?" and Peter responded affirmatively, Jesus said for the third time, *"Feed my sheep"* (emphasis mine).

Did you notice that Jesus never asked Peter if he loved sheep? You'll begin to love sheep when you love the Savior enough to get involved with the sheep. It's not our love for the lost that first motivates us to pray for them or to evangelize them. It is our love for the Savior. As we embrace love for the Savior, His love begins to permeate our lives and we, as laborers in the harvest, glorify Him.

God Works through Our Prayers

The second reason we can be confident in our praying for lost sinners is the realization that God has chosen to do His work through our prayers.[2] God could save lost sinners apart from our praying for them or sharing the gospel, but He has chosen not to do so.

How, then, can they call on the one they have not believed in? And how can they believe in the one of whom they have not heard? And how can they hear without someone preaching to them?[3]

FREE WILL

Some suggest that it does no good to pray for lost sinners because it violates their free will. First of all, we need to address the issue of free will. In reality, no one has a free will because all of our wills have been affected by our heritage, our biology, our environment, and more. What we really mean is that God won't violate our moral responsibility.

Historically, there have been two major misunderstandings that have paralyzed confident praying for lost sinners. First, there are some who are afraid of offending God's sovereignty. They conclude that God is so sovereign that He will save who He wants to save and He doesn't need the help of mortal man. For us to evangelize or pray for lost sinners would be to get in the way of a sovereign God who elects those whom He chooses, based on His own foreknowledge and mercy. Those who hold this view would not allow a place for people to be involved in the process since that would be offending God's sovereignty.

On the other hand, there are those who are afraid of offending each individual's sovereignty. They're so afraid they might do something that violates individual moral responsibility that they are afraid to ask God to influence others. They conclude that if they ask God to influence people, He will interfere with their moral choice. Some would compromise the issue by asking God to influence others to some degree, but not enough to cause them to make a choice one way or the other.

We can be sure that God will never violate His own design in creation. He has designed that each of us be responsible for our choices. On the other hand, God does not rob himself of His own sovereignty. He has commanded us to be participants in His ruling of this universe, and we are to do that through prayer and obedience. It is perfectly in line with the word of God as revealed in Scripture for us to pray that God not only slightly influence lost sinners toward Him, but also for us to pray confidently that God will save sinners. John Piper defines sovereignty as "the right and power of God to elect and then bring hardened sinners to faith and salvation."[4]

HOW DO WE PRAY FOR THE LOST?

How then should we pray for lost sinners? According to the direction of Jesus, the savior of lost sinners, we are to pray for laborers to be sent into the harvest field.[5] This verse, again, indicates that God has chosen not to save sinners apart from the presentation of the gospel. Second, we are to pray for the blinding power of Satan to be bound and for eyes to be opened to the glory of the gospel.

And even if our gospel is veiled, it is veiled to those who are perishing. The god of this age has blinded the minds of unbelievers, so that they cannot see the light of the gospel of the glory of Christ, who is the image of God. For we do not preach ourselves, but Jesus Christ as Lord, and ourselves as your servants for Jesus' sake.[6]

When Jesus sent out the seventy-two, He instructed them to go with the authority that He himself had been given by the Father.[7] The disciples came back, astounded that they had authority even over demons. Jesus explained that His authority was transferred to the disciples, His representatives on earth. We too have been given the authority of Christ. In prayer, our authority is exercised against the schemes of the devil, who seeks to blind people's eyes to the reality of their need for salvation and the provision that's been made in Jesus Christ. As we pray, binding this power of Satan and asking for God's mercy in opening their eyes, our prayers become effective in the specific area of warfare.

Years ago, I ran across a little tract called *How I Learned to Pray for the Lost.* The tract was built around the first two sentences of the Scripture passage quoted above, 2 Corinthians 4:3–4. In trying to implement those truths, I encouraged the youth I was working with at the time to make a list of their lost friends and then pray boldly that their friends' blind eyes would be opened by the power of God, and that Satan's inroad to these lives would be shut off. Then I encouraged them to be sensitive to the leadership of the Holy Spirit, who would show them how to replace the lies of the devil with the truths of God's word.

I encouraged them to offer to take these people to lunch or serve them in some other way, to always look for an open door of opportunity to share a word of truth. This method of evangelism superseded the "salesmanship approach," which usually included a cold call on a prospect where we read them a set of Scriptures and sought to get them to pray a prayer on the spot. Many times, in God's mercy, this salesmanship approach worked, but we found an even greater measure of fruitfulness in praying and then obeying.

The apostle Paul seemed to have an understanding of the double-barreled approach to seeing the kingdom of God manifested on earth. He prayed for people's eyes to be opened and then preached the word of God, knowing that the truth has to replace the lies in order for people to be liberated. We find a common methodology in his epistles, where he teaches a little, then "prays it in," and then teaches some more. Why should we believe that we can improve on this methodology? Our ministry to lost sinners must include prayers and the ministry of the Word of Truth.

Pray for an Undivided Heart

A third insight into praying for sinners is found in Ezekiel 11:19. Oftentimes, when we pray for individuals, we discover that their hearts are divided. That is, they have a tenderness in their heart toward God, yet they seem to be holding on to some other source of security or significance. This Scripture encourages us to pray that God will give them an undivided heart and put a new spirit within them, removing the old heart of flesh.

I will give them an undivided heart and put a new spirit in them;

I will remove from them their heart of stone and give them a heart of flesh.[8]

Pray for God's Mercy

Fourth, it is always right that we pray for God's mercy to be shown to those who deserve wrath. In Ezekiel 36, God explains that His people have experienced His wrath because they defiled His name among the nations. He will reclaim the reputation of His name by showing mercy to His people and restoring them to a position of blessedness:

> "'For I will take you out of the nations; I will gather you from all the countries and bring you back into your own land. I will sprinkle clean water on you, and you will be clean; I will cleanse you from all your impurities and from all your idols. I will give you a new heart and put a new spirit in you; I will remove from you your heart of stone and give you a heart of flesh. And I will put my Spirit in you and move you to follow my decrees and be careful to keep my laws.'"[9]

Repentance Is a Gift from God

The fifth encouragement we have in praying for lost sinners can be found in 2 Timothy:

> And the Lord's servant must not quarrel; instead, he must be kind to everyone, able to teach, not resentful. Those who oppose

him he must gently instruct, in the hope that God will grant them repentance leading them to a knowledge of the truth, and that they will come to their senses and escape from the trap of the devil, who has taken them captive to do his will.[10]

In this passage, we are reminded that repentance is a gift from God. We rely on God's mercy to grant the repentance to those who are confused, blind, and lost.

Release the Living Word of God

The sixth and last instruction regarding praying for lost sinners includes the prayer to release the Living Word of God. We've already discussed in Romans 10:9–13 that God has chosen not to save sinners apart from the preaching and receiving of the word of God. His word created life, His word sustains it, and His word will consummate it. Therefore, His word accomplishes everything that God does. Our prayers and lives must always be consistent with this word—otherwise they are inconsistent with the government of God.

We are encouraged by Scripture that the weapons we use are not weapons of the world. Our weapons have divine power. They are able to demolish strongholds, to demolish arguments and every pretension that sets itself up against the knowledge of God. The weapons we have are prayer and the proclamation of the word of God. The stronghold of truth destroys the stronghold of lies. That which shuts the mouth of arguments against God is God's argument itself. All the ideologies and theories that have been promoted by man will ultimately fall, and God's word will remain standing. God's eternal word is His instrument to accomplish all He intends to do on the earth; therefore, we must be emissaries that carry out the word by example and proclamation.

> Finally, brothers, pray for us that the message of the Lord may spread rapidly and be honored, just as it was with you. And pray that we may be delivered from wicked and evil men.[11]

We have some part in the speed at which the word of God spreads. If it were not so, we would not be encouraged to pray that it would happen. The race is on! The ideas of man, many of which originate from hell,[12] race against the word of God. We know the ultimate winner, but we get to have some influence for our generation.

Instead of complaining about the spread of relativism and humanism, we could spend our time praying for the rapid spread of the word of God. It will always win when given a chance to compete. So, with our passionate prayers, we must enter truth into the race.

God loves sinners! God gives authority to believers to proclaim light to blind eyes. God gives His word to dispel the lies that bind sinners. God's Spirit will convict when truth is presented. God wants more laborers in the harvest field. God's word will win the race against all other ideologies— if it is entered by us. There is an abundance of lightning and thunder in heaven waiting for our incense. Let's get it moved from heaven to earth.

PRAYING FOR PRODIGALS

If anyone sees his brother commit a sin that does not lead to death,
he should pray and God will give him life.
I refer to those whose sin does not lead to death.
There is a sin that leads to death.
I am not saying that he should pray about that.

1 JOHN 5:16

The heaviest burdens are borne by those who care deeply about a loved one who is living outside of God's promises. One of the main areas of concern for Christians is the overall welfare of the children of God; we know we must pray for them as well as for conversion of lost sinners. Wandering children are a problem. In this context I use "children" to refer to spiritual children, those belonging to the family of God.

The burden is at least doubled when the spiritual child who is wandering is also a natural child.

We are all too aware that the battle is not over in prayer when the sinner converts to be a child of God. In fact, most of the prayers in the New Testament are not for the sinners, but for the children who need to progress in their relationship with God. If lost sinners need the mixture of prayer and proclamation of the word for their eyes to be opened in order to be converted, certainly immature, or wayward, believers need the mixture of prayer and the word of God in order to overcome the obstacles that might be preventing them from enjoying their journey with Christ.

God Loves the Lost

How do we pray for wayward, spiritual children? First, we are encouraged by the biblical revelation that God's attention is on those who are away. In Luke, chapter 15, we find God's attitude toward lost things. Jesus talks about the one lost sheep out of the hundred, with the message that the ninety-nine are left so the one can be found. He then tells the story about a lost coin. His major point is the priority that's given to finding it. Then He tells about lost sons.

In this familiar passage that we commonly call the parable of the prodigal son, we see again the father's attitude toward that which is out of place. Instead of the father being offended by the insolence and rebellion of his younger son, we find him always ready to receive him, aggressively running to bestow restored fellowship when the son shows signs of repentance. In the case of the second son of that story, we find the father out in the servants' quarters, pleading with the self-righteous son to give up his self-righteousness and to come enjoy the fellowship of grace.

God loves His children. To hear some explanations of God's attitude toward Christians who sin, we might conclude that God loves lost sinners more than He loves saved saints.

I can remember a time in my journey when I sought desperately to prove to myself that my first conversion experience had failed. It would've made me feel better to know that some of the selfish things I'd done had been done prior to my true conversion. If I could only prove that my first profession was faulty, then I could explain the sinfulness of my post-conversion days. I was sure that God would forgive an ignorant sinner, but I wasn't so sure that He would forgive a wayward son.

Many times, we in the church have made sinning saints feel so embarrassed and ashamed because of their sinful choices that they've found no encouragement to repent. At the same time, we have magnified greatly the stories of those who committed terrible crimes. We are able to accept them because their crimes were done "before conversion."

We should make no mistake—God hates all sin, pre-conversion and post-conversion. But the wonderful truth of the gospel is that the blood of Jesus Christ forgives us of all our sin.

But if we walk in the light, as he is in the light, we have fellowship with one another, and the blood of Jesus, his Son, purifies us from all sin.[1]

Pray with Confidence for Sinning Christians

Second, we are encouraged by Scripture to pray for sinning Christians:

> If anyone sees his brother commit a sin that does not lead to
> death, he should pray and God will give him life. I refer to those
> whose sin does not lead to death. There is a sin that leads to
> death. I am not saying that he should pray about that. All wrong-
> doing is sin, and there is sin that does not lead to death.[2]

Oftentimes, Bible students so focus on their efforts to define "sin that leads to death" that they miss the point of the passage. John is saying that it is our privilege and responsibility, when seeing another Christian sin, to pray with confidence. When we do, we are assured that God will give life to that brother or sister.

It's hard to imagine what kind of health would surge through the body of Christ if believers took this encouragement to pray seriously. Instead of criticizing when we see another sin, we should pray. When one Christian criticizes or mocks another who is confused about his or her walk with God, it is an obvious symptom of a sick church. Healthy brothers and sisters do not rejoice over the failures of their siblings

It seems, today, that some have concluded that their first responsi-bility when they see a Christian sin is to expose it, sometimes without even confronting that person. Jesus made it clear that when someone sins, we are first to go privately to that brother or sister. If there is no repentance or reconciliation, then and only then are we to take witnesses.

If the matter is still not settled, then it is to be taken to the church (not to the media and not to the world). What if we believed that when we saw fellow Christians sinning, we could pray and God would actually intervene in their lives, saving them from the destruction of sin and the body of Christ from disillusionment and embarrassment?

> "If your brother sins against you, go and show him his fault, just between the two of you. If he listens to you, you have won your brother over. But if he will not listen, take one or two others along so that 'every matter may be established by the testimony of two or three witnesses.' If he refuses to listen to them, tell it to the church; and if he refuses to listen even to the church, treat him as you would a pagan or a tax collector.
>
> "I tell you the truth, whatever you bind on earth will be bound in heaven, and whatever you loose on earth will be loosed in heaven.
>
> "Again, I tell you that if two of you on earth agree about anything you ask for, it will be done for you by my Father in heaven. For where two or three come together in my name, there am I with them."[3]

The only limitation that John puts on this kind of confident praying for sinning brothers and sisters is if we see someone commit a "sin that leads to death." But what is the sin that leads to death? Since John doesn't explain it to us in detail, we must assume that his readers would have understood from the context of his letter.

Throughout the letter John talks about those who claim to be believers, but who have bought into a Gnostic heresy and are repudiating and denouncing the fact that Jesus, the Son of God, has come in the flesh. This would be consistent with the writer of Hebrews, who states that those who choose to reject Jesus as God's way to salvation have no further recourse in coming to God.[4]

God isn't going to make two ways to come to Him. He has, once and for all, settled that faith in Jesus Christ alone is the only acceptable way to reconciliation with God. John says that if we see someone who openly renounces God's only way to salvation, we have no confidence that praying for him will grant life. Notice that John doesn't prohibit this kind of prayer, he simply says we won't have the same level of confidence. We might be able to pray with great passion as we would for any rebellious sinner, but we won't have the confidence that accompanies those praying for Christians who are sinning.

Pray without Fainting

Third, God encourages us to pray without fainting. In Luke, chapter 18, Jesus tells a parable specifically for the purpose of showing us how to pray and not give up.[5] Obviously, Jesus knew that fainting would be a possibility for those of us who represent heaven in this world.

This is the familiar story about a woman who kept coming to a judge and asking that the judge grant justice against her adversary. For a while he refused, but he finally gave in because she continued to bother him. Jesus takes a clue from the unjust judge and tells a story of contrast:

And the Lord said, "Listen to what the unjust judge says. And will not God bring about justice for his chosen ones, who cry out to him day and night? Will he keep putting them off? I tell you, he will see that they get justice, and quickly. However, when the Son of Man comes, will he find faith on the earth?"[6]

Jesus is saying to those disciples who want to know how to pray and not give up that, in contrast to the judge in the story, the heavenly Father doesn't have to be pestered into answering prayer. Because He loves his elect and He loves justice, He will bring about their requests speedily.

Some, in trying to interpret this parable of Jesus, have concluded that Jesus is teaching us to be persistent in pestering God—that if we pray enough times, God will finally conclude that we're serious or that He's never going to get rid of us until He answers. That was the nature of the unjust judge. It is not the nature of our heavenly Father. There are four important phrases in this parable that help us in our endeavor to be persistent in our prayers.

GOD'S CHOSEN ONES

First, *chosen ones*—instead of our being just an impersonal woman who has a problem with an adversary, we are God's "chosen ones." He has chosen us to be not only His children, but also His friends. In choosing us to be His friends, He has promised that He will not only tell us what to do (the message that servants get), but also what He is doing.

"I no longer call you servants, because a servant does not know his master's business. Instead, I have called you friends, for everything that I learned from my Father I have made known to you."[7]

As chosen ones, we have been given the privilege and responsibility to represent Him on earth. His full attention is given to us. We are not some foreigners who are coming to Him to ask for that which He has not promised. He has committed Himself to us and is willing to act in our behalf as we act in His behalf.

GOD PROMISES JUSTICE

Second, we will *get justice.* The widow was looking for justice from the unjust judge. God promises justice to His chosen ones. Justice enforces the laws of the government that is in control. For us to understand the justice that God will enforce in our behalf, we need to understand the constitution of that government. It's found in Hebrews 8:

"This is the covenant I will make with the house of Israel after that time, declares the Lord. I will put my laws in their minds and write them on their hearts. I will be their God, and they will be my people. No longer will a man teach his neighbor, or a man his brother, saying, 'Know the Lord,' because they will all know me, from the least of them to the greatest. For I will forgive their wickedness and will remember their sins no more."[8]

This is the justice that God is interested in instituting in our behalf. "I will put my laws in their minds and write them on their hearts." It is God's will and determination to move us from external motivation to internal motivation. In giving us the indwelling Holy Spirit, He fulfills this aspect of His government by putting His laws into our minds and within our hearts. That is, He causes us to know His will and even gives us the desire to do it.

This is an aspect of justice that we can ask for and claim, that He has promised to give. "I will be their God, and they will be my people." There is, in this promise, the satisfaction of our need to belong and be significant. God has promised that He will be responsible for our protection, provision, and guidance; that He alone is our God and is willing to identify with us. He is not ashamed to be called our God.

God also states, "They will all know me." He is promising again that He will answer prayers relating to His revealing Himself to us. No longer do we have to depend upon teachers to give God's ways to us. He does it Himself, through His own specific revelation of Himself.

Then God says, "I will forgive their wickedness and will remember their sins no more." He has chosen not to hold our sins against us. He can remember anything; He has chosen not to remember our sins. Because of that, as long as we trust His word, we have continual access to Him. When the adversary comes to accuse us before God and ourselves, to bring condemnation and shame, we have the right to claim these aspects of God's covenant with us.

GOD ACTS QUICKLY

The third element that draws our attention in Jesus' remarks after the parable of the unjust judge is the word *quickly.* This can be a confounding term. Quickly by whose time, since our life is but a vapor and, in God's economy, a thousand years can be like one day? What does quickly mean? In our minds, quickly means sometime within the next twenty-four-hour period or, certainly, within the next week. Yet God is willing to work not in just years, but in centuries. When God gave Abraham promises about his heritage, He told Abraham that his bloodline would be successful, but that somewhere in the midst of it would be four hundred years of slavery to a foreign power. Even today as we read about Israel's stay in Egypt for four hundred years, it doesn't seem so bad...unless you were Israel and lived under the heavy hand of a pharaoh for a long time.

One of our great obstacles to overcoming fainting in prayer is our definition of *quickly.* We must be willing for God to give definition to the word. We can be sure that His answer will be done as quickly as we can handle it and still fulfill His purposes—but after all, as we discussed before, our first desire is that He be glorified and that His will be done on earth as it is in heaven. Obviously, we want our pressure relieved. But as children of the kingdom, we are willing to stay under the pressure in order for God's quickly to be accomplished.

FAITH THAT LASTS

The last phrase that grabs our attention after the parable of the unjust judge is, *When the Son of Man comes, will he find faith on the earth?* The issue of the timing of God's answers will certainly bring periods of testing to our patience and perseverance. To the chosen one who understands the heart of the Father, persistence in prayer does not depend on how quickly the answer comes, but on the surety that it shall.

The Prodigal Son

When our son David was a senior in college, he came home one weekend to inform our family that he was, essentially, renouncing the way of life that we had taught him and the values on which we had based our lives. He was choosing to follow some of the ways of the existentialist philosophers of his day and the humanistic lifestyle that accompanied such thinking. He wasn't sure what he believed, but he was sure that what we believed was narrow-minded, exclusive, and based on religious prejudice. After delivering his declaration to his mother, his sister, and me, he was picked up by some friends who were sympathetic with his point of view.

There are no words to express the pain that struck in our hearts like lightning as the car rolled away from our driveway. For a long time, the pain was too severe to express—and then it came forth in wails and groans and buckets of tears. What had we done wrong? Where could we have missed it so badly? Why was this happening to us? Does this disqualify us from any venue of ministry? Those and hundreds of other questions flooded our minds as parents.

We tried to communicate with our son, but it was obvious we were speaking two different languages. It became clear that nothing we could

say was going to persuade him to change his mind. We knew that all we
could do was pray.

As I studied the different Scriptures in the New Testament on prayer,
this teaching of Jesus in Luke 18 grabbed my heart. My commitment to
the Lord was that I, like that persistent widow, was going to continue
asking for His intervention until I got the answer or until time was up
for me. I enlisted the prayers of many others around the country, and
many other precious saints felt the need to pray and prayed without
knowing the specifics of the situation. Based on the insights of this parable of the persistent widow, I prayed many times a day like this:

Heavenly Father, I know You're not an unjust judge and that I
do not have to pester You into hearing me. I am one of your
chosen ones. I thank you for choosing me to be your son and
your representative on the earth. I have been the victim of an
assault by an adversary who is seeking to steal my son and yours.
I am asking that You would intervene quickly and grant justice
in this case. I am praying that You will put your laws into his
mind and into his heart, replacing the deception that has entered
there. I am praying that You will be his God and defend him
against all others who are trying to replace You. I am asking You
to make him know You by special revelation of Yourself, and I
am praying that You would forgive his wickedness and remember his sins no more. And Father, I realize that your "quickly"
and my "quickly" may not mean the same thing, but I can only

operate on the time that I live in, and it is short. So, I am asking You to do this today, and I believe that You shall. And I am asking that if You can't do it today, do it tomorrow. In Jesus' name. Amen."

For two years I prayed these words at least daily, sometimes many times during the day. My commitment was to pray that prayer for the rest of my life or until I saw the answer. Someone listening in on my prayer might think it foolish for me to say, "I'm asking for it today, and if not today, tomorrow," but I was committed that, if the Father should choose to delay my answer and return before I died, He would find me on my knees praying that prayer. I was committed to answer the question that Jesus asked at the end of the parable, "When the Son of Man comes, will He find faith on the earth?" My answer was and is a resounding *"Yes!"*

Approximately two years after our son's declaration of independence, he came back to me and said, "Dad, I don't know what I believe, but I think you know what you believe. So until I can find out what I believe, I will submit to you."

I tried not to show all the emotion that I felt, but at that moment, I knew justice was beginning to be done. I knew that my son probably didn't understand that when he submitted to God's delegated authority, he was submitting to God.

In a matter of weeks, David submitted himself to a discipleship program in Big Fork, Montana. In those beautiful mountains of Montana he discovered afresh an intimacy with God that his heart longed for, but his mind couldn't comprehend. Today my son works with me in ministry and is being used greatly by God to influence his generation to be passionately in love with the Lord Jesus and to find their destiny in the kingdom of God.

With every ounce of energy in me, I give praise to the heavenly Father who answers His chosen ones quickly. I also join with each father and mother who, today, continues to pray that prayer of faith. I will stay with them on my knees, praying that God will answer today, and if not today, then tomorrow. I will rejoice with all who get the answer in their hearts and in their hands, and I will continue to pray with those who wait for God's "quickly" to come to pass.

IT'S SIMPLER
THAN YOU THINK

"'Call to me and I will answer you and tell you great and
unsearchable things you do not know.'"

JEREMIAH 33:3

I have always been impressed with the profound simplicity of God's ways. His ways are beyond discovery for the proud heart, but obvious and simple to those who love Him.

"Call" is His invitation! How complicated is that? In any language, from any place, in any condition—just call. It doesn't have to be pretty or profound. There is no requirement on verbiage or virtue—just call.

Call when you're happy and rejoice in His blessings. Call when you're sad and find His comfort. Call when you're guilty and bathe in His cleansing. Call when you're depressed and hear His voice of encouragement. Call when your world is upside down and watch Him reveal new worlds to you. Call when the burden is heavy and the Holy Spirit will come and pray for you. Call when your strength is too little and your faith is too weak. He will mount you on eagles' wings so that you "will run and not grow weary, [you] will walk and not be faint."[1] Call when your heart is too full of praise to be expressed in known language. He will send a choir of angels to help you praise His name. Call! That's our part. There is never an inappropriate time to call if done in faith.

"I will answer you" is His part. He wants to answer because He is the answer. He answers by giving Himself to the caller. His answer will never be less than expected. It might be so much more that we can't identify it, but it will not be less than we ask for. "Great and unsearchable things" should not surprise us. When God gives Himself, we can't comprehend what we see.

Our second prayer should always be: "Lord, give me eyes to see the answer You have given to my first prayer."

While the rest of the world is searching for man's dignity in his independence, we already have the dignity to manage the world through prayer. We are heaven's representatives on earth, who have a perfect Man in heaven representing us. Our Father still has a plan for this earth to be a dwelling place for His glory. We get to send up the smoke, and He delights to mix it with His fire and send it back to earth. What a privilege to be part of God's co-op called incense and thunder.

References

Appel, Pat. *Nine Great American Myths.* Brentwood, Tenn.: Wolgemuth & Hyatt Publishers, 1991.

Barna, George. *The Second Coming of the Church.* Nashville, Tenn., London, Vancouver, Melbourne: World Publishing, 1982.

Billheimer, Paul E. *Destined for the Throne.* Port Washington, Penn.: Christian Literature Crusade, 1975.

Carre, E. G., ed. *Praying Hyde.* South Plainfield, N.J.: Bridge Publishing, 1982.

Crabb, Larry. *Understanding People.* Grand Rapids, Mich.: Zondervan Publishing, 1987.

Forsyth, P. T. *The Soul of Prayer.* Salem, Ohio: Schmul Publishing Company, 1986.

Grudem, Wayne. *Systematic Theology.* Grand Rapids, Mich.: Zondervan Publishing, 1994.

Huegel, F. J. *The Ministry of Intercession.* Minneapolis, Minn.: Bethany Fellowship, 1971.

Jones, E. Stanley. *The Unshakable Kingdom and the Unchanging Person.* Bellingham, Wash.: McNett Press, 1995.

Nelson, Allan E. *Broken in the Right Place.* Nashville, Tenn.: Thomas Nelson Publishers, 1994.

Piper, John. *The Pleasures of God.* Portland, Ore.: Multnomah Press, 1991.

Sampson, Steve. *I Was Always on My Mind.* England: Sovereign World Publishers, 1996.

Watts, Brian. *The Treasure in the Field.* Langley, British Columbia, Canada: Imogen Resources, 1995.

Notes

INTRODUCTION

1. James 5:17
2. Acts 12:5

CHAPTER ONE

1. P. T. Forsyth, *The Soul of Prayer* (London: Charles H. Kelly, 1916), 9.
2. John 13:31–16
3. John 14:12
4. John 17:4
5. John 17:6
6. Steve Sampson, *I Was Always on My Mind* (England: Sovereign World Publishers, 1996).
7. John 16:26–27
8. John 16:24
9. John 17:1

CHAPTER TWO

1. Matthew 6:9–10
2. Revelation 1:3
3. Revelation 5:8
4. Revelation 8:1–5
5. Psalm 18:6
6. Psalm 18:7–19
7. Acts 2:42
8. Acts 2:43–44
9. Acts 4:24–26
10. Acts 4:31

11. Acts 6:7

12. Acts 9:3–6

13. Acts 10:4–5

14. Acts 12:5

15. Acts 12:13–16

16. Acts 12:23–24

17. Acts 13:2–3

18. Acts 16:25–26

19. Acts 21:5–6

20. Acts 27:22–26

21. Acts 28:31

22. John 14:20–21

23. John 15:7–8

24. John 15:9

25. John 15:10

26. John 15:16

27. John 17:11–12

28. Psalm 118:10

29. Psalm 118:11–14

CHAPTER THREE

1. Larry Crabb, *Understanding People* (Grand Rapids, Mich.: Zondervan, 1987), 16.

2. John 14:12–14

3. Judges 3:1–2

4. John 14:14

5. Hebrews 1:1–3

6. Luke 18:11

7. Luke 10:27

8. Luke 10:28

9. Luke 10:29
10. Matthew 10:7–8
11. Luke 10:30–37
12. Luke 7:36–50
13. Matthew 6:1–6
14. Luke 15:11–32
15. Matthew 21:33–46
16. Matthew 21:45–56
17. John 9:36
18. Isaiah 59:1–2
19. Romans 6:23
20. Hebrews 10:14
21. Hebrews 10:19
22. Romans 8:1
23. 1 John 3:18–22 (NASB)
24. 1 Corinthians 10:23
25. 1 John 3:18–20

CHAPTER FOUR
1. Romans 1:1 (NASB)
2. James 1:1 (NASB)
3. 2 Peter 1:1 (NASB)
4. Matthew 11:28–30
5. Genesis 3:10
6. Deuteronomy 18:20–22
7. Numbers 14:44
8. Numbers 16:3
9. Numbers 16:1–35
10. Matthew 23
11. Matthew 23:11

12. Luke 12:16–21

13. James 4:13–14

14. Luke 18:9–14

15. Isaiah 66:1–2

16. James 1:26–27

17. Matthew 5:3

18. Donald McCollough, *Discipleship Journal* (1989), 49, quoted in Allan E. Nelson, *Broken in the Right Place* (Nashville, Tenn.: Thomas Nelson Publishers, 1994), 52.

19. Psalm 32:8–9

20. Watchman Nee, *The Spiritual Man* (New York City: Christian Fellowship Publications, 1968), quoted in Allan E. Nelson, *Broken,* 56.

21. Hebrews 13:12

22. Psalm 51:17

CHAPTER FIVE

1. Rosemary Rutland, "Dog Collars and Spiked Bracelets" *Powerline* newsletter 22, no. 4 (October 1998). Used by permission of the author.

2. 1 John 3:21–22

3. 1 John 5:14–15

4. Genesis 1:26–27

5. Romans 11:36

6. John 2:1–11

7. Romans 5:9–10

8. 1 Corinthians 2:12

9. John 10:26

10. Genesis 15:16

11. 1 John 5:16

12. Matthew 6:9–13

13. Ephesians 1:5–6

14. Psalm 50:15

15. Joshua 2:8–24

16. Psalm 50:15

17. Hebrews 4:3

18. 2 Chronicles 16:9

CHAPTER SIX

1. Acts 2:29–36

2. Peter J. Leithart, *The Kingdom and the Power* (Phillipsburg, N.J.: P&R Publishing, 1993), 49.

3. Matthew 28:18–20

4. Matthew 25:14–30

5. Matthew 13:3–9

6. 2 Corinthians 4:3–4

7. Pat Appel, *Nine Great American Myths* (Brentwood, Tenn.: Wolgemuth & Hyatt Publishers, 1991).

8. Ibid, 127.

9. Ibid, 81.

10. Vance Packard, *The Hidden Persuaders,* quoted in Pat Appel, *Nine Great American Myths,* 10, from a quote in R.W. Stott, *Between Two Worlds* (Grand Rapids, Mich.: William B. Eerdmans Publishing Company, 1982), 174.

11. Matthew 13:22

CHAPTER SEVEN

1. Daniel 2:44

2. Matthew 3:2

3. Matthew 4:17

4. Matthew 5–7

5. John 14:12

6. Acts 28:23

7. Hebrews 11:1, 6

8. Romans 5:5

9. Matthew 24:36–25:46

10. Genesis 1:28

11. Ezekiel 36:6–12; Daniel 4:21–22; Ezekiel 37:23; Brian Watts, *Treasure in the Field* (Langley, British Columbia, Canada: Imogen, 1995), 89.

12. Acts 4:23–31

13. Brian Watts, *Treasure in the Field*, 89.

14. G. K. Chesterton, *The Everlasting Man* (London: Harter and Stoughton, People's Library Edition, 1927), 206. Quoted in Brian Watts, *Treasure in the Field*, 105.

CHAPTER EIGHT

1. Psalm 107:20

2. Luke 4:18–19; Isaiah 61:1–3

3. Isaiah 9:7

4. Proverbs 16:7

5. Proverbs 20:20

6. Proverbs 30:11

7. George Barna, *The Second Coming of the Church* (Nashville, London, Vancouver, Melbourne: World Publishing, 1982), 38.

8. 1 Timothy 5:1–12

9. Colossians 3:15

10. Philippians 4:4–9

11. Matthew 6:33

CHAPTER NINE

1. Matthew 11:25–27
2. James 1:26–27
3. Isaiah 58:1–14
4. 1 Kings 18:20–40
5. James 5:4–6
6. 1 Timothy 1:12–15
7. Deuteronomy 28:1

CHAPTER TEN

1. Romans 8:26
2. 1 Corinthians 6:17
3. Romans 8:11
4. Romans 8:15
5. Romans 8:16
6. Romans 8:26
7. 1 Corinthians 2:11–12
8. Ephesians 3:14–16
9. 1 Corinthians 14:1
10. 1 Corinthians 14:2
11. 1 Corinthians 14:4

CHAPTER ELEVEN

1. 2 Corinthians 5:18–20
2. Matthew 14:22–33
3. Hebrews 7:25
4. Romans 9:3
5. John 1:19–28
6. Mark 11:22–25
7. John 15:5
8. Mark 9:24

9. Mark 11:24

10. Hebrews 4:3

CHAPTER TWELVE

1. John 21:1–19

2. John 14:12–14

3. Romans 10:14

4. John Piper, *The Pleasures of God* (Portland, Ore.: Multnomah Press, 1991), 227.

5. Matthew 9:38

6. 2 Corinthians 4:3–5

7. Luke 10:1–2

8. Ezekiel 11:19

9. Ezekiel 36:24–27

10. 2 Timothy 2:24–26

11. 2 Thessalonians 3:1–2

12. James 3:13–16

CHAPTER THIRTEEN

1. 1 John 1:7

2. 1 John 5:16–17

3. Matthew 18:15–20

4. Hebrews 6:4–6

5. Luke 18:1–5

6. Luke 18:6–8

7. John 15:15

8. Hebrews 8:10–12

EPILOGUE

1. Isaiah 40:31